Sacha you are beautiful on the inside and the outside. Believing with you for all your dreams to come true

Avril

BIG DREAMS
DON'T JUST HAPPEN

◆ FriesenPress

Suite 300 - 990 Fort St
Victoria, BC, V8V 3K2
Canada

www.friesenpress.com

Big Dreams Don't Just Happen

Copyright © 2018 by Avril Riley
First Edition — 2018

All rights reserved. No part of this publication may be reproduced, distributed, or transmitted in any form or by any means, including photocopying, scanning, uploading, recording, or other electronic or mechanical methods of sharing, without the permission of the author. If you would like to use material from the book (other than for review purposes), prior written permission must be obtained by contacting the author at permissions@avrilriley.com. Thank you for your support of the author's rights.

Cataloguing data available from Library and Archives Canada

The Author is not responsible for websites (or their content) that are not owned by the Author.

Photo cover credits The Boho House | Cover design Optmedia Creative Studio

To order additional copies, visit:
www.avrilriley.com
www.books.friesenpress.com/store

For more information:
Email: author@avrilriley.com
www.avrilriley.com

ISBN
978-1-5255-1639-9 (Hardcover)
978-1-5255-1640-5 (Paperback)
978-1-5255-1641-2 (eBook)

Distributed to the trade by The Ingram Book Company

CHALLENGE THE STATUS QUO

BIG DREAMS
DON'T JUST HAPPEN

RE-NEW YOUR MIND.
RE-ENVISION YOUR FUTURE.
RE-DEFINE YOUR GOALS.

This book is dedicated to

Zeris Graham, my beloved mother
and
Rufus Riley, my wonderful husband

You are both
my unconditional supporters
my empathetic enablers
the voices of wisdom
the coaches in my corner
my cheerleaders
and the wind beneath my wings

Without your unconditional love, patience, and support this vision would not have been possible.

TABLE OF CONTENTS

Acknowledgements ix
Introduction xiii
Chapter One: Pursue Personal Mastery 1
Chapter Two: Challenge the Status Quo 11
Chapter Three: Re-New Your Mind 29
Chapter Four: Re-Envision Your Future 61
Chapter Five: Re-Define Your Goals 87
Chapter Six: Lead from the Future 99
Notes 121
Glossary 131

ACKNOWLEDGEMENTS

Special thanks to:

Dr. Pat Francis, my mentor and coach, for the many words of wisdom and guidance. You have allowed me to stand tall on your shoulders.
My sisters and brother for always being there; my niece and nephew Abigail and Aunri Beckford for those cuddly hugs, which are refreshing;
Francine Britt-Bowman from (Chicago), Illinois for the initial editing of the manuscript;
My CHAYIL Power Group from Rwanda, South Africa, Canada, (Buffalo) New York, (Chicago) Illinois, and Hawaii for keeping the fire of glory ablaze as I embarked on this project.

BIG DREAMS
DON'T JUST HAPPEN

INTRODUCTION

Personal mastery is one of the most powerful terms a leader can include in their vocabulary. It describes a discipline of personal growth and learning and conveys unlimited greatness. "Personal" indicates something that starts from within oneself and flows outwards. It implies switching on the internal light and connecting with one's values, identity, emotions, motives, goals, and becoming self-aware. "Mastery" implies competence, commitment, achievement, learning, vision, purpose, resilience, and opportunities. Mastery is not a destination but a journey, which will last a lifetime and be filled with lifelong growth and development. It is something every leader should desire and pursue in their "business of life."

What does personal mastery have to do with leaders? A leader in this book is anyone who is responsible for shaping and creating their desired future. Every individual is accountable for being committed to their vision and growth; this makes you a leader of yourself, a role you must master before leading others. Personal mastery is founded on several principles:

- Clarity of vision.
- Lifelong learning.

- Creative tension.
- Commitment to the truth.
- Being grounded in competence and skills.
- Disciplined personal growth and learning.
- Continually focusing and refocusing on what you truly desire.
- The ability to focus on both intrinsic desires and secondary goals.
- The ability to accomplish complex tasks with grace and ease.

These principles are important for leaders to apply to achieve success. Looking at life as a business offers a fresh perspective that complements personal mastery. This concept is based on the idea that each person should approach and manage their life in the same way a corporation conducts its business affairs. An organization has assets and liabilities, vision, mission, values, and goals. The organizational leaders use different approaches to review their competitive edge.

Like the organization each person has strengths, gifts, knowledge, skills, and talents, which are their personal intellectual assets. Each person also possesses psychological assets; these include hope, optimism, resilience, confidence, and a growth mindset. In addition, you have liabilities which are things that limit your capabilities, such as disempowering beliefs, fixed mindsets and intellectual gaps.

The gap between where you are now (current reality) and where you want to be (your vision) is understood by conducting a personal strengths, weaknesses, opportunities, and threats (SWOT) analysis. The SWOT analysis will take into consideration your assets and liabilities. The world is experiencing rapid changes in digital transformation, disruptive technologies, changing consumer demands, globalization, and social connectedness making it important for leaders to be self-aware. The SWOT analysis will identify threats and opportunities in your business of life in this changing world. Leaders must understand this new concept of managing your life as a business to remain relevant as they pursue personal mastery.

Since you are reading this book, I believe you have the desire to understand personal mastery. You have the desire to be clear about your vision and your current reality, to live in the present and prepare for the future. To get there, you need to recognize patterns of status quo that must be challenged, constantly renew your mind, foster new self-awareness, continuously listen to the future to detect emerging trends and patterns, envision or re-envision your future, and create new goals. Goals, by their nature, are designed to have an end date, but growth is forever. In this book, I encourage you to create a vision that is focused both on your goals, which are guaranteed to end, and personal growth, which lasts a lifetime. This process is introduced in the **6 Steps Growth Goal Model™**.

To achieve your purpose, you must develop a growth plan. I will share with you my personal stories, struggles, setbacks, and victories as I journeyed in my business of life. During the peaks and valleys, understanding and leveraging my intellectual and psychological assets was crucial in fostering positive personal development. This book is my effort and contribution to help you grow, and tap into your potentials to become all that you were created to be. Your dreams and visions must be activated to serve your purpose.

Bob Johansen, Distinguished Fellow with the Institute for the Future (IFTF) and author of *Leaders Make the Future*, uses the military term VUCA to describe the world as Volatile, Uncertain, Complex, and Ambiguous. To remain relevant in a VUCA world, leaders must be willing to release the past, manage the present, scan and sense the future for emerging trends, continuously re-envision the plans for their life and look for ways to adopt the new. I encourage you to follow the steps in this book and dream big, wisely, to create a growth strategy. My desire is that you will leverage the principles and actions I've used, implement them in your own life, and create your stories of transformation and destiny.

As you create a vision for your life and chart the course, my goal is to help you develop the right strategies, and for you to live with eternity in mind. When you read this book, I recommend you find a quiet place and use a reflection journal, record your thoughts, decide what will be different for you, what will change for you, and incorporate any lessons learned into your business of life.

Success has a story. I've shared my personal failures and success stories with you; now pay it forward and create an accountability group. Share this book with your friends and family by reading and discussing each chapter. My dream is that everyone will intentionally pursue personal mastery and growth as they manage their business of life. I pray you will continue to learn, unlearn, tweak, and update your growth

INTRODUCTION

plan as hindsight drives the releasing of the past and foresight drives insight into pursuing the future in the present. Big dreams don't just happen—they are intentionally designed.

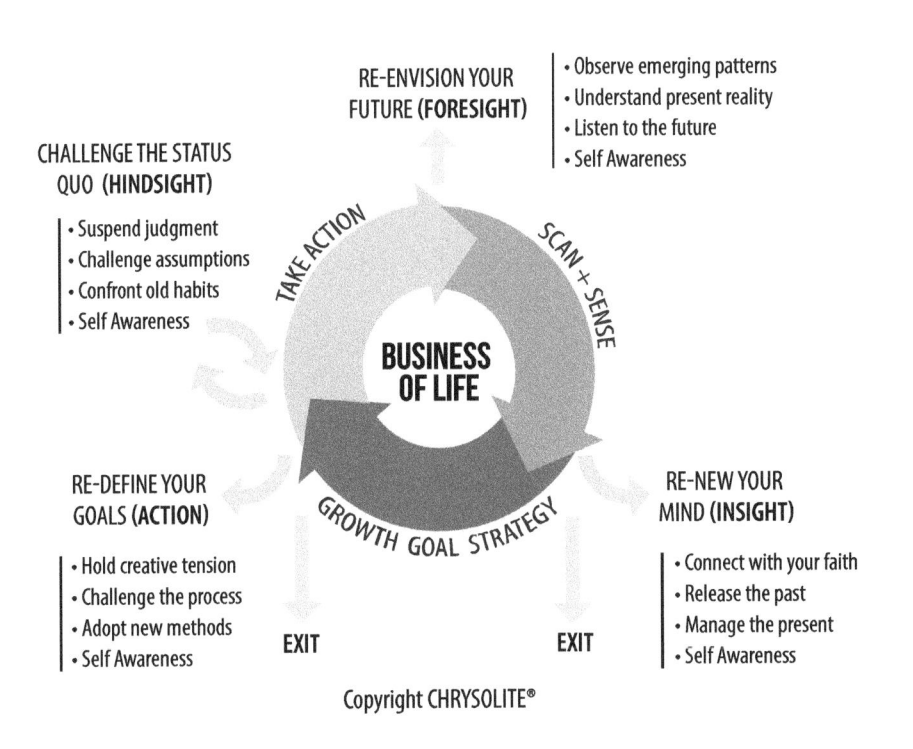

RE-ENVISION YOUR FUTURE (FORESIGHT)
- Observe emerging patterns
- Understand present reality
- Listen to the future
- Self Awareness

CHALLENGE THE STATUS QUO (HINDSIGHT)
- Suspend judgment
- Challenge assumptions
- Confront old habits
- Self Awareness

RE-DEFINE YOUR GOALS (ACTION)
- Hold creative tension
- Challenge the process
- Adopt new methods
- Self Awareness

RE-NEW YOUR MIND (INSIGHT)
- Connect with your faith
- Release the past
- Manage the present
- Self Awareness

TAKE ACTION · SCAN + SENSE · GROWTH GOAL STRATEGY

BUSINESS OF LIFE

EXIT   EXIT

Copyright CHRYSOLITE®

CHAPTER ONE
PURSUE PERSONAL MASTERY

"To respect and claim your perspective while simultaneously being open to other perspectives is the key to learning." —Dr. Ron Short

In spring 2008 I caught a glimpse of my future. I reflected on and assessed past realities, captured the hindsight where patterns of status quo existed in my life, managed my present, and went deeper to gain valuable insights. I looked outwards and relied heavily on foresight as I began pursuing personal mastery and growth. I breathed in the fresh spring air and watched flower shoots pushing to break free from the soil. Spring symbolizes renewal, birth, hope, growth, and promise. The time had arrived for my seeds of potential to be cultivated, but where would I begin? Like the flower seed buried deep in the soil, the first place for me to look was inside.

My curiosity was at an all-time high because I was stepping into the world of entrepreneurship, forging a collaborative business relationship to launch my production agency. There were many uncertainties, including the risk of investing without a guaranteed financial return. I listened to the rhythm of my current realities, faced the mental models that formed my habits, and analyzed my values and belief systems, which influenced my decisions and behaviors. The sounds I heard formed a symphony influenced by my faith, my experiences, and the people and places engaged in shaping and reshaping my reality.

My passion for learning propelled me to create a map of the peaks and valleys in my business of life to discover my fertile place. The fertile place within me had an abundance of dormant assets, representing extensive seeds of potentials and opportunities. I kept shining a light within myself; like peeling an onion, layers of my life were removed, exposing my psychological resources (wisdom, optimism, confidence, hope), intellectual assets (knowledge, skills, competence, strengths), and the force of faith that brought me through the peaks and valleys.

Inside of me were seeds of potentials: unlimited assets waiting to be invested, as well as liabilities that needed to be eliminated. My reflective journey revealed the subtle human system that influences my behavior and my vision for the future. I felt a heightened sense of self-awareness; having been down this path in the past, I knew it was time for change. For change to be possible, I had to embrace a new self-awareness, new self-regulation, and an understanding of future trends and digital patterns.

Curiosity gave me a new level of courage to challenge my status quo, my current state of affair and seek new opportunities. I wanted to do something different, see from a new perspective, and create something extraordinary. I was in pursuit of personal mastery. That year, 2008, with the support, guidance, and encouragement of my dear friend Dorothy, I successfully launched my events production company. This was my second entrepreneurial initiative.

I read the inspiring story of Jessica Cox, born in Arizona without arms due to a rare birth defect. This was Cox's reality, which she accepted. Cox did not have the use of her hands to drive a car or pump her own gas. She stopped using prosthetic arms at age fourteen and mastered the art of using her feet to do activities like these.

This is an incredible story of a woman who obviously was exceptionally self-aware. She leveraged her strength to unveil seeds of potentials and created her desired future. At the tender age of ten, Cox became engaged in the sport of taekwondo. She earned her first black belt at fourteen and won the Arizona State Championship in 2014. Cox graduated from the University of Arizona with a psychology major.

In 2005, Cox took to the air, passionately pursuing her vision of becoming a licensed pilot. Using her feet, she flew a single-engine airplane via Wright Flight. Three years of training passed as Cox mastered controlling the airplane yoke and throttle with her feet. On October 10, 2008, Cox earned her sport pilot license and became the world's first licensed armless pilot.

No doubt, Cox had to overcome any limiting beliefs in her mind. One thing we can conclude from her story is that she had a growth mindset and believed nothing was impossible.

In the pursuit of your vision you will encounter setbacks

and challenges. Cox could have perceived her situation as impossible. She could have submitted to the pressures and tensions pushing against her vision of becoming a pilot. However, with resiliency and relentless pursuit, Cox vision became a reality. During this process, did she constantly renew her mind and embrace new patterns of thinking? One thing is evident: Cox adapted with grace to her circumstances and pushed past limiting beliefs.

There had to be a shift in Cox's mindset. Cox understood the impact her decisions and actions would have on her future. One of the many lessons of Cox's story is her response to, and awareness of her limitations. Self-awareness is required to overcome challenges, but what Cox also possessed was the ability to transform threats into opportunities, leverage her strengths, use creativity, practice resiliency, and explore opportunities in situations that appeared to put her at a disadvantage.

Cox's success story is powerful and exemplifies clarity of vision, purpose, and well-defined goals. Cox could have chosen to remain stuck in the present reality of being armless, but she understood the power and strength of her feet and utilized her capabilities to create new realities. Her life offers a tremendous example of core leadership qualities: personal visioning, adaptability, flexibility, creativity, and resiliency.

Cox drew from her reservoir of strength to pursue her vision, and created her reality. Living without arms was not the enemy. It became a force that ignited clarity of vision, greatness, and shaped her purpose-driven future. Something on the inside was awakened and she became unstoppable.

Psychiatrist Carl Jung expressed the idea of vision and self-awareness when he stated, "Your vision will become clear only when you look into your heart. Who looks outside, dreams. Who looks inside, awakens." Many of us yearn to understand our purpose and spend precious time seeking this knowledge on the outside. It starts within you.

Who you were truly created to be will never be understood and discovered until you begin looking on the inside and connecting with your faith to ignite your spiritual power. Countless times, I've asked my friends, peers, or employees the question "Who are you?" The response is usually a chuckle, blank stare, silence, an earful of numerous professional accomplishments, or the history of a family lineage. The outward focus overshadows the inward focus, dimming the ability to flick on the internal switch and see what truly lies at the core of one's being.

Reflecting on Cox's remarkable story and my personal journey to entrepreneurship, I gained insights into a central theme flowing through both stories. There is a commitment to learning, vision, self-awareness and growth. This commitment is referred to as personal mastery. Peter Senge, in *The Fifth Discipline*, defines personal mastery as "the discipline of continually clarifying and deepening our personal vision, of focusing our energies, of developing patience, and seeing reality objectively." In describing people with significant levels of personal mastery, Senge asserts, "People with a high-levels of personal mastery are able to consistently realize the results that matter most deeply to them—in effect, they approach their life as an artist would approach a work of art.

They achieve this by commitment to lifelong learning."

Do you know what matters most to you? How committed are you to investing in your learning? Do you approach your life intentionally or are you reacting as curveballs get thrown at you?

Scientist George Washington Carver said, "No individual has any right to come into the world and go out of it without leaving behind him distinct and legitimate reasons for having passed through it." Why are you here? What is your purpose? What is your passion? Who are you?

What driving forces made Jessica Cox defy all odds, challenge herself beyond personal limitations and norms, and break free from disempowering beliefs to achieve her vision? It appears Cox was committed to the truth. Senge describes the concept of commitment to the truth as "a relentless willingness to root out the ways we limit or deceive ourselves from seeing what is, and to continually challenge our theories of why things are the way they are."

Living a life that is constantly evolving starts with personal awareness: an awareness of who we are, the desires of our hearts, and the visions our hearts long to experience. These visions are capable of surviving the harsh winter and bursting through the soil to grow and flourish. Personal mastery demands resilience, managing creative tensions, and seeing realities. Personal mastery demands lifelong learning, and clarifying personal visions and values, which are fundamental to achieving success. Perhaps if this process is understood, visions that never made it to fruition would not be perceived as failures but as opportunities to learn something new.

Intrigued by what constitutes the essence of personal mastery, I conducted a social media survey to ask my friends across the globe, "What does personal mastery mean to you?"

Joseph Arden Valerio, from the Philippines, responded, "Personal mastery is being able to evaluate one's self. It is being able to understand how we think and why we do the things we do, having clarity around our purpose and direction in life." Joseph focused on the thinking process, the whys of our actions, and clarity of purpose. The quest for personal mastery demands self-control of your patterns of thinking, because your thoughts will drive your emotions and behaviors. Faulty thinking will cause you to go in a different direction from your vision.

Donna Gordon-Mitchell, my high school friend from Jamaica, expressed her view, "Personal mastery means adjusting to my ever-changing environment to stay the course to achieve my goals. This is tough but I'm resilient. Kids need to go to college and be supported the whole way before I retire to Jamaica." The keywords Donna expressed in her perspective on personal mastery are "ever-changing," "goals," and "resilient." Donna's vision and goals are clear. She is ensuring that her actions in the present will create a future in which her children will have access to education before she retires. Donna also recognizes that her environment is not static and will draw on her leadership competency of being resilient to navigate changes.

Charlene Pineda, my dear friend from graduate school and executive coach, shared, "A core, foundational piece of personal mastery is the ability to really see and reckon with one's shadow side, getting to a place of acceptance about the things that can be changed and those that can't, and eventually getting to a place of self-management, regardless of context."

The central theme among these responses was learning. Joseph recognized that self-awareness is crucial for success. Donna's learning experience included adapting to an ever-changing environment and Charlene acknowledged learning self-management and getting to a place of acceptance and embracing changes. These common themes are fundamental to personal mastery and the process of re-envisioning the future.

Learning is key. Inside our subconscious, we all have the desire to learn. We spend our lives learning. Learning how to walk. Learning how to swim. Learning to love. Now we are in a digital era and we will need to learn how to lead from the future as we pursue personal mastery. We consistently expand our minds and capacities by learning new things with the aim of realizing our greatest goals and producing extraordinary results.

The responses from the social media survey confirmed Senge's perspective on personal mastery. It is a discipline in which learners deepen and clarify their personal vision. They are committed to personal growth and development, and continually learn to see reality more clearly. Your energy will be focused on the things that are truly important, which ensures you remain committed to the pathways you have chosen. This is a discipline that enables you to flow with the process of time as patience is developed and reality is viewed objectively. Personal mastery includes being able to pause, reflect, suspend your judgements and assumptions, and recognize patterns and habits that limit you and leave you stuck in the past.

Achieving personal mastery is a life-long process. The operative word is *process* (versus something you finally possess or attain). Mediocrity has no place in your life. You've been designed for mastery, coded for greatness and wired with purpose. You are the master of your life, get clear about it! There are four components to use as guidelines to manage this business of life.

- Challenge the Status Quo.
- Re-New Your Mind.
- Re-Envision Your Future.
- Re-Define Your Goals.

These are constant cycles in the pursuit of personal and leadership growth. Spring 2008 marked a new beginning for me, and I have to manage my business of life.

Big Dreams Don't Just Happen
Fundamentals of Personal Mastery

Leaders who are growing in personal mastery exhibit the characteristics listed below. In pursuit of personal mastery, use this checklist as a reminder of the core principles and check to see if you are growing in these principles.

- Understand your purpose.
- Pursue spiritual growth.

- Pursue lifelong learning.
- Manage your emotions.
- Clarify your personal vision.
- Commit to personal growth.
- Remain true to your vision.
- Remain committed to the truth.
- Achieve tasks with grace and ease.
- Be accountable for your experiences.
- Focus on results and see current reality.
- Develop the ability to suspend your judgement.
- Intentionally develop your skills and competencies.
- Clarify your understanding of your current reality.
- Develop the ability to recognize patterns and cycles.
- Lead from the future.

CHAPTER TWO
CHALLENGE THE STATUS QUO

"Insanity is doing the same things over and over again and expecting different results." —Unknown.

The word "status quo" finds its root in Latin; it refers to the existing state of affair. Every leader should intentionally avoid slipping into a state of status quo where growth and development stops. There is a fable about boiling a frog. If you drop a frog into boiling water, instinctively it will jump out. On the other hand, if you take that same frog and place it into a pot of cool water and slowly increase the temperature, the frog will be oblivious to the water gradually getting hotter. The water temperature will continue to increase and the frog will sit there until the water boils, and boil with it. Life gets cloudy in the pot until the frog is unable to escape. The moral of the story is that settling into routines and habits will create a state of status quo. It is easy to detect sudden environmental threats but hard to be aware of threats that arise slowly. If you are not listening to the future, changes will sneak up on you.

When you hear "status quo," what imagery or thoughts are conjured up in your mind? We are living in a digital age where the world is rapidly changing. We are being invaded by digital disruption and social change—innovative ideas, objects, and social patterns. The rapid speed and volatile force with which technology is changing is impacting humanity. We are no longer confined by geographical borders, which have given rise to globalization. The world is shrinking and cultures are being integrated. Internationalization is on the rise and it is now easier for organizations to do business in other nations. Cognitive systems are being designed to function similar to the human brain – learning, processing, thinking, reasoning, analyzing and making decisions. How we live, work, play, shop, communicate, build relationships, consume products, utilize services and trade is undergoing cycles of rapid change. There is no room for contentment, and doing the same things in the same way. Maintaining the status quo will not chart the course or create the blueprint for future success. Digital and cognitive disruptions, globalization and internationalization are the new norms.

Whether you perceive yourself as an individual, organizational leader, owner of a business, or an entrepreneur, you are a leader. A leader in this context is anyone who has the sole responsibility for shaping and directing the events of their past, present, and future business of life. Many leaders are failing to see the glaring warning signs of current and future changes. They are sleeping, unaware of the social and technological movements that are changing the world. Dr. Martin Luther King Jr. stated, "Today, our very survival depends on our ability to stay awake, to adjust to new ideas, to remain vigilant and to face the challenge of change." You

CHALLENGE THE STATUS QUO

were born with greatness inside of you. When you rise to the call of personal leadership, challenge the status quo, and tap into your faith, you will awaken the greatness within you.

Lifelong learning is fundamental to pursuing personal mastery and personal development. Maintaining the status quo will never be an option because yesterday's success is old news. In my consulting practice, I've often heard the forbidden words, "We have always done it this way" or "Why do we have to change? We did it this way for many years." These words are evidence of leaders who are stuck in the past and their current reality. They lack the ability to gain fresh insights, operate with an open mind, and embrace new opportunities. Leaders who are settled in a culture that fosters maintaining the status quo are unwilling to abandon traditional views, systems, and processes. They operate with a stagnant mentality and refuse to embrace the idea of learning new competencies. Their mindsets are stuck in the past, and they are forever celebrating past accomplishments. They fail at managing the present and embracing the future.

In 1997, when Steve Jobs returned to Apple Inc., he launched the "Think Different" campaign. Jobs was known for being a big thinker who never settled for the status quo. In one of his famous speeches, Steve toasted those he refers to as the "crazy ones": "Here's to the crazy ones. The misfits. The rebels. The troublemakers. The round pegs in the square holes. The ones who see things differently. They're not fond of rules. And they have no respect for the status quo. You can quote them, disagree with them, glorify or vilify them. About the only thing you can't do is ignore them. Because they change things. They push the human race forward. And while some may see them as the crazy ones, we see genius. Because the people who are crazy enough to think they can change the world, are the ones who do."

This generation is forcing everyone to think and lead differently. They are creating products and services that are shaping the global community. Many leaders are engaged in countless discussions about this group; however, they are sitting back and watching this transformation emerge without challenging their personal status quo and vision. If leaders choose to let the future unfold by default, the consequences could be devastating. Leaders may find themselves counted in the unemployment statistics. They may be competing against those Jobs refers to as "troublemakers," "misfits," and "rebels" for employment.

The Automation and Artificial Intelligence (AI) revolution has arrived and are classified as significant disruptive forces that is challenging the status quo. In a recent Gallup Business Journal article captioned, "3 Trends That Will Disrupt Your Workplace Forever," authors Andrew Dugan and Bailey Nelson wrote about the rapid changes of AI and automation that has left leaders wondering: *"What will workplaces look like in the future, and how are those differences affecting my workplace now?"* "How susceptible are leaders to robotic replacement and computerisation?"

The Gallup analysis referenced in this article revealed that, "Millennials are the generation most vulnerable to the threat of AI and automation." Thirty-seven percent of millennials faces the possibility of being replaced by AI and automation. Trailing behind are the older generation at thirty-two percent. Regardless of your generation category, how will you prepare for an AI-driven and computerised future? Passivity is not an option. Status quo is not an option.

Leaders must seriously challenge their status quo and think about their current and future educational plans, the nature of careers, leadership and businesses in the future. The absence of sensing change, and taking action will result in leaders becoming irrelevant.

Organizations are not so very different from individuals. History has recorded the demise of organizations that failed to challenge the status quo. Nortel Networks Corporation (also known as Nortel), established in Montreal, Quebec, in 1895, once dominated the telecommunications and data networking equipment market. At the peak of its existence, Nortel employees totalled 94,500 globally and the company held more than a third of the total valuation of all the companies listed on the Toronto Stock Exchange. In June 2009, however, Nortel filed one of the largest bankruptcy cases known in Canada.

The marketplace was changing rapidly, competition was rising and "clearly" Nortel had demonstrated a remarkable deficiency in moving the firm forward. In the online Financial Post, writer Jamie Sturgeon in the article "Where Nortel Went Wrong," quoted *Ottawa Citizen* business columnist James Bagnall citing, "The R&D labs that had produced the world's first all-digital phone network and won the race to dominate fibre-optics in 2000 had descended into mediocrity." How did a powerful telecom equipment giant become mediocre and irrelevant? As leaders, this is an example of a question we need to ask ourselves as we navigate our business of life. What are your personal, career, leadership and business strategies? How do you plan to grow, compete and thrive in the digital, and AI-driven world?

The status quo must be challenged in all dimensions of life. With personal mastery grounded in competencies and skills, leaders must be aware of their psychological and intellectual assets. To remain relevant and marketable in the present and the future, intentionally challenge your education and expertise. Be quick to identify gaps in your psychological and intellectual assets by assessing them against current and future demands, then take actions to close those gaps. This is not a one-time procedure; it is a lifelong and evolving process.

If you are a business owner, your products, services, and business model are core elements that must consistently evolve. The business space, in which you operate as well as consumer behaviors and preferences, will not remain the same. Change is inevitable and leaders must adopt new skills, boldly explore to find new innovations, and be agile in getting them into the hands of consumers.

The business of life in the twenty-first century calls for leaders to shape their future with resiliency, creativity, adaptability, and agility. Their passion for innovation must enable them to meet the personal and business challenges of this digital age. Boldness, courage, and collaboration must replace fear and resistance and become the new norm. Now is the time for leaders and organizations to challenge the status quo, foster innovation, encourage collaboration, and dig deeper into the issues that could influence their future relevance. The act of challenging the status quo is the first evidence that you are ready to go on a journey to dream big, ignite change, and create your future.

Challenging the Status Quo

"Influential people are never satisfied with the status quo. They're the ones who constantly ask, 'What if?' and 'Why not?' They're not afraid to challenge conventional wisdom, and they don't disrupt things for the sake of being disruptive; they do it to make things better." —Travis Bradberry

Challenging the status quo will expose areas in your personal life, career, leadership, or business that are dormant and lack growth. These are areas where you have shifted into cruise control and still expect to land the next top job, climb the corporate ladder, or land the next big contract. Challenging the status quo means making decisions and taking actions to shift from normal and constant routines. Challenging the status quo means looking at the processes and procedures (methods) used in executing your vision, a personal or business function to determine if they are outdated. Methods and processes used in execution that are no longer relevant will not yield the expected outcomes. A strategy must exist to identify and update outdated methods and processes. Leaders must have a strategy for personal growth with eyes that look towards the future. Leaders must have innovative ways of conducting this business of life that enables them to thrive and survive in a complex and changing world. Bold choices and agile decisions must be made, and risks must be taken to transform challenges into innovative solutions. Challenging the status quo is a practice of growth and development, with the goal of producing the results needed to remain relevant in a complex world. When you challenge the status quo, you have decided to abandon traditional perspectives and adopt insightful ways to create new opportunities. Instead of being stuck in the past, leaders will leverage hindsight to understand and appreciate the past, and use the insights gained to manage the present.

Principles of Challenging the Status Quo

"If you want to thrive in today's economy, you must challenge the status quo and get the financial education necessary to succeed." —Robert Kiyosaki

Our human system is comprised of our beliefs, values, thoughts, and emotions, which play a crucial role during change. As the human mind analyzes and interprets systems, people, and events, it sends out signals that engage our thought processes. The mind uses its powers to receive the incoming signals and create emotions. During periods of change, these emotions can be associated with fear of failure or fear of change, which can hold you hostage in a stagnant state. Your emotions will trigger behavioral responses, which produce results. You are accountable for these results, which could be either embracing the new or exiting the growth process.

Every human being is guided by a belief system, which determines the way they view the world, people, and themselves. Your approach to change will be driven by your internal compass (core beliefs), which influences your desire to evolve and grow from the inside out. Another component of your internal compass is your values. Your values determine the things you hold dear and believe are important in the way you live and work in the business of life. Values determine your priorities and serve as a gauge to tell you if you are living the life you desire. Your thoughts, which are influenced by your beliefs and values, drive your emotions, and your emotions drive your behavior. When your actions align with your beliefs and values, emotional satisfaction is attained.

When you willingly challenge the status quo, you will discover empowering beliefs and values that drive the positive emotional states needed to embrace change. Change will always result in doing something differently. It is impossible for growth to occur within the comfort zone. When resistance sets in, it's because your negative emotions are engaged. Leaders who challenge the status quo do so because of their desire to learn and grow. This is important in pursuit of personal mastery because personal mastery is a disciplined commitment to growth and development. For growth and development to occur, there must be an end to looking toward the past, stretching, shifting to focus on managing the present, sensing and scanning of the future.

There are four principles to be considered when challenging the status quo.

- **Principle 1:** Suspend Judgement. Challenge Assumptions
- **Principle 2:** Be Open-Minded. Be Curious
- **Principle 3:** Shift from Habits. Sense Emerging Patterns
- **Principle 4:** Be Accountable for Your Growth

Principle 1
Suspend Judgement. Challenge Assumptions

"The challenge of the unknown future is so much more exciting than the stories of the accomplished past." —Simon Sinek

Judgements and assumptions are factors that inhibit growth. Assumptions may be that the problem is already understood, the answer is known, and there is nothing new to gain from exploration. We often become attached to our assumptions, and will go to great lengths to passionately defend them. In 1985 an incident occurred which forever influenced Coca-Cola thinking. The organization changed the fabled secret formula for Coca-Cola and introduce the "New Coke" brand. The events which took place the Spring and Summer of 1985 were dubbed as the "marketing blunder of the century." Consumers hoarded the "old" Coke; there were cries of protest as people chanted "We want the real thing."

Coca-Cola assumed its consumers would embrace the "New Coke" brand. However, following the protest they challenged that assumption which triggered a brand reversal and a new brand launch of "Coca-Cola Classic." Challenging your assumptions enables you to change your perspectives on past accomplishments, change your mindset about current situations you may be experiencing, and future opportunities.

When judgements are suspended, you open yourself to learn and see reality from a fresh and diverse perspective versus being stuck in mental models and habits. Judging what is being actioned or communicated will suppress learning opportunities and impede understanding. The absence of understanding will lead to assumptions that will take you down a rabbit trail. On the rabbit trail, your brain recalls past experiences and knowledge, including any assumptions and biases you may hold. Your brain will extrapolate these elements to interpret the situation and inaccurately predict potential outcomes. In narrow-minded leaders this will suppress creativity, a skill required to lead from the future. To enable the flow of creativity, suspend your voice of judgement, challenge your assumptions, and question the things you take for granted. In pursuit of personal mastery avoid spending time down pathways that will lead to dead ends.

Principle 2
Be Open-Minded. Be Curious

"Be curious enough to keep an open mind to what's happening around you in society. You can look at yourself and the world at the same time." —Jochen Zeitz

It is easy for a leader to ease into the comfort zone when things are going well. The presence of peace and stability, however, is never an indication not to challenge the status quo. Learning is lifelong, and opportunities for growth will consistently present themselves. In this business of life, regardless of the dimension I am focusing on, there are two approaches I use to challenge the status quo. First, I nurture a curious mind and remain open-minded. Secondly, I probe what I am hearing, sensing, and observing by using open-ended questions. I analyze and interpret the data collected to make sense of what is happening and what needs to happen.

The power of using questions to challenge the status quo can never be contested. The first question to ask yourself is: "How will I benefit from the status quo?" The second question is: "What is holding me back?" The third question is: "Do I fear failure?"

Questions will provide insights into the areas of your life where comfort zones exist. Which ones are creating a haven and need to be disturbed? What mindsets, values, and beliefs are supporting those comfort zones? With an open mind and an open heart, asking open-ended questions during conversations will provide detailed responses and reveal deep insights.

In *Theory U*, Otto Scharmer describes an open heart as "the capacity for empathic listening, for appreciative inquiry, and for 'exchanging places' with another person or system." As you engage in empathetic conversations you will become aware that the outward appearance of someone else may not necessarily reflect their inner condition or state of mind.

Otto describes having an open mind as "the capacity to see with fresh eyes, to inquire and reflect." Being curious and having an open mind engages active listening, without a rebuttal argument being at the forefront of your thoughts. It is important to have an open mind to ensure that when insights are being revealed you do not push back defensively, because this will block your learning. In moments of learning defensive attitudes will foster an atmosphere where you operate on the surface instead of getting to the root of issues that contributes to status quo.

Principle 3
Shift from Habits. Sense Emerging Patterns

"A world filled with opportunities is waiting. Change your habits. Change your thinking." —Avril Riley

Everyone has a daily routine they follow and for most it's consistent. You wake up in the morning, spend time connecting with your faith dimension, check your emails, throw in a healthy dose of exercise, get the kids ready for school, get dressed for work, navigate the busy roads to arrive on time, manage the affairs of your career, drive home after a long day at the office, relax and unwind, check your emails, catch up on your favorite shows, connect with your family and friends, get dressed for bed, sleep, wake up the next morning, and repeat the cycle, perhaps with some variation.

These habits can be subtle and robotic. I'm always amused at my behavior driving to the office and back home. I get into the car and start the engine. Without giving any thought to what I should do next, I find myself merging onto the highway, taking a specific exit, and turning into the driveway at the office. This happens automatically because these are repetitive actions, which are programmed in my mind and have become ingrained neurologically.

To shift from habits to sensing emerging patterns requires considering all aspects of your life. Challenge your status quo by taking the time to reflect on and observe your daily routines. Search for patterns in your thought processes and behaviors as you conduct your daily routines at home, at the office, and as you engage others. What patterns can you detect by observing how you get the kids ready for school or how you manage the affairs of your career? What does your daily interaction with others at work reveal about your psychological and intellectual assets? Be observant of your surroundings. Be curious. Seek to understand how the outcome of the events taking place in proximity to you will potentially have an impact on you. Begin to expand your thinking beyond the pattern of known habits. If you are not in touch with your habits you will be blinded by those habits. You will become stuck in traditions, failing to clarify current reality and see new opportunities.

Challenging the status quo includes understanding your habits. Inside your world of habits is a new world filled with possibilities waiting to be discovered.

Principle 4
Be Accountable for Your Growth

"Faith is taking the first step even when you don't see the whole staircase." —Dr. Martin Luther King Jr.

Forces of change continue to emerge in the digital era, and challenging the status quo is a decision that only you can make for yourself. Each leader is accountable for their learning, growth, and development. You are accountable for recognizing the shift in workplace designs, the way in which you collaborate, communicate, consume and share digital space. With an open mind, you must be accountable for sensing new patterns of change by engaging in daily reflection, hindsight, insight, and foresight.

Making the decision to challenge the status quo and seeing through diverse lenses will yield the benefit of identifying habits that are candidates for change. Leaders must be committed to eliminating the old ways of existence, when they are exposed, and preparing to embrace the new. Living with purpose and connecting to a cause that is greater than you require clarity of vision. Living with purpose will never be accomplished with a status quo mindset. It will never be attained if you do not invest in personal growth and development.

Once there is an awareness of your habits and patterns you are accountable for establishing a growth plan, executing the growth plan, and engaging in cycles of evaluation. Unfortunately, many leaders never reach the point of planning and their growth stops. However, leaders who are accountable for their growth are competent at listening, seeing, scanning, sensing, and adapting to current and future conditions. They demonstrate high-level of self-awareness and diligently pursue personal mastery.

This business of life is conducted by being very intentional in your actions. If you are settled in a place of contentment, then you have chosen to live a life by intentional default rather than intentional design. Your intentional design will be supported by creative forces, which will push you along your defined blueprint. It will attract creative forces and power to help move you along the journey. If you choose not to challenge the status quo, then you have decided to exit the process of learning and growing.

Life may have dealt you cards plagued with setbacks and disappointments, but the power to exchange those cards, rise above the status quo, and intentionally design your life is in your hands. Eleanor Roosevelt once said, "One's philosophy is not best expressed in words; it is expressed in the choices one makes. In stopping to think through the meaning of what I have learned, there is much that I believe intensely, much I am unsure of. In the long run, we shape our lives and we shape ourselves. The process never ends until we die. And, the choices we make are ultimately our own responsibility." Where are you now? Are you operating by default, waiting for movements in the world to decide what actions should be taken, or are you proactively preparing for the future?

Big Dreams Don't Just Happen
Action Plan to Re-Think the Status Quo

Are there areas in your business of life where you are stuck in a state of status quo? To answer this question, use the checklist below to conduct a self-diagnosis to assess if you are living by intentional default or intentional design. If you find yourself straddling both sides or scoring higher on the intentional default side, then you are a prime candidate for personal, career and leadership growth.

INTENTIONAL DEFAULT	INTENTIONAL DESIGN
• Think small.	• Think big.
• Failure means wrong choices.	• Failure means opportunity.
• Play it safe. Be risk-adverse.	• Take risks.
• Fear of failure mindset.	• Freedom to fail mindset.
• Knowledge is capital.	• Share knowledge.
• Give up easily.	• Persevere under pressure.
• Problems are barriers.	• Problems are stepping-stones.
• Change is risky business.	• Change is opportunity.
• Learning will end.	• Learning is lifelong.
• Talk more. Listen less.	• Listen more. Talk less.
• Procrastinate.	• Seize the moment and take action.
• Diversity fosters chaos.	• Diversity fosters innovation.
• Have a fixed mindset.	• Have a growth mindset.
• Resist digital platforms.	• Embrace digital platforms.
• Unaware of intellectual gaps.	• Aware of intellectual gaps.
• Unaware of psychological gaps.	• Aware of psychological gaps.
• Do not have a formal growth plan.	• Have a formal growth plan.

CHAPTER THREE
RE-NEW YOUR MIND

"The greatest revolution of our generation is that human beings, by changing the inner attitudes of their minds, can change the outer aspects of their life." —Marilyn Ferguson

The greatest challenges we will encounter are the many wars that take place inside our mind. Your mind is a battlefield where wars are initiated and fought, resulting in either victories or defeats. No one desires to go through unpleasant life experiences, but they do occur. Depending on your response, in those moments of pain there are opportunities to gain glory. Life is filled with ups and downs, twists, turns, and curves. I've had my share of fighting wars on the battlefield of my mind.

In this business of life, I've experienced failures, setbacks, betrayals, and disappointments. Drawing from my source of power and tapping into my faith, I've remained resilient and responded with a growth mindset. The moments of pain I experienced became a lifetime of ever-increasing glory. John McDonnell, the retired head coach for the University of Arkansas Razorbacks track team, once said, "Every problem introduces a person to himself." Profound and true.

An unpleasant experience during the early days of my information technology career introduced me to me. It began when my career as a software developer was at its peak. Junior in experience but passionate and driven, I was empowered to provide technical team leadership to a small team for a software development initiative with a Fortune 500 organization. This shift in my status quo came with great accountability. I embraced the opportunity and stepped out to encounter the unknowns and risks. However, I did not sense the major career changes that were coming to disrupt my routine as a developer. In the absence of foresight, I was unprepared for the future. I was focused on managing the present but failed to listen to the future.

My experience as a technical team lead was successful. I received many prestigious accolades. This experience set the stage to introduce me to a special person: me. My emotions of happiness and confidence were at an all-time high; I was leading me and leading others. I was living my purpose.

My joy soon became moments of pain, and an opportunity for growth. A position became available in management, and I was encouraged by my mentor to apply. When my application was made public I was scoffed at, endured listening to the voices of critics who deemed I was incapable of being a leader. I was blatantly discouraged from applying, and was told there were other qualified candidates. I thank Jesus Christ for my coaches because I ignored the voices of cynicism and went full speed ahead with the process. I was selected as one of the potential candidates, survived many rounds of interviews and was offered the position. The next series of events were defining moments in my business of life.

Hot on the heels of my promotion to leadership was the first deliverable: to collaborate with a third-party solution provider on a multimillion-dollar initiative. The initiative was complex and large-scaled, with global partners, multiple vendors, and a project team peaking up to eighty-five resources. Did I mention the many new things we had to learn and implement? Yes, this initiative became the model for several new processes, procedures, and methodologies, with new team members and a rookie manager blended into the mix. Could my learning curve be any bigger? At this point, I was the development manager providing people leadership. A logical mind would have thought my role as the development manager was sufficient.

My adrenaline was racing at the speed of light. Despite the number of new elements that were included, I was ready to challenge my leadership status quo. Challenging the status quo began as a battle in my mind between what I believed I could do versus the steep odds of success with all these new undertakings. The initiative was complex but with my growth mindset I was determined to win this battle.

During the formation of the project team, the consulting agency who licensed the third-party solution believed the employees were not capable of successfully executing the product integration activities. I acknowledged they were the experts but this belief violated my core values of trust and respect. There was another perspective; a passionate rookie leader who dared to think and believe differently was bold enough to challenge the status quo. I created a proposal for providing leadership to the project team, including resources from the consulting organization, and presented it to management for approval.

The rookie manager was on a mission and with a specific request. I had a vision of the future and sought the opportunity to be entrusted with greater leadership responsibilities. I was confident of my competencies and ability to complete this project within the timeframe the "big guns" had promised.

Etched in my mind was the image of me drawing on the whiteboard as I illustrated the proposed project strategy. There was a learning and development strategy, which focused on enhancing the technical knowledge of the team; a peer coaching strategy to ensure all team members were set up for success; a strategy that ensured each software discipline had a team lead; a mentorship strategy aimed at ensuring the team leads would be mentored by the consultants; an infusion strategy that entailed a floor plan outlining the co-locating of the full-time employees with the consultants for the purposes of knowledge transfer. The final strategy was the project management approach to manage the deliverables. Brilliant! I had all the strategies in place—but I neglected to create the most important strategy: employee engagement.

I remembered the silence that followed my proposal, and then the response: *"If you are bold enough to present this proposal then you are bold enough to take on the project leadership role."* The accountability and trust were now mine. I had to deliver what my mind envisioned and my voice breathed life into. I was now accountable for the rules of the game.

I could have chosen the path of mediocrity or renewed my mind and mindsets to achieve another step towards my true purpose. I was confident that I was destined to become a world leader of people and organizations. My desire is to be a leader who would effect positive changes in the lives of others but this vision was challenged. In this business of life there are always opportunities and challenges; you are accountable for your responses and actions.

The Leadership Challenge

"Crisis reveals your character and the response to the crisis shapes your future." —Avril Riley

The stage was set. Actors were in place. Curtains were drawn and the show began with the rookie manager as the lead actress. We were pressured by time, a huge learning curve, and consultants who had little confidence in our capabilities. I had to grow up fast. From listening to the weekly tears of an employee who may have felt incompetent, to managing those who were overly confident and saw no value in coaching, as well as encouraging those who were knowledgeable and moving along fine, and managing our offshore resources, I had a full plate.

Time was ticking and I had to find a way to make this work. The answer was evident (so I thought): this called for "taking charge." At that time, I had no knowledge this style of leadership is referred to as "command and control." I had envisioned a perfect world where the team was successful but I did not pause to fully assess the costs and consequences of my decisions. I was a rookie manager and did not understand that the command and control leadership style cannot command commitment. Commitment is inspired. I was unaware that this style of leadership did not integrate with transformational efforts. This style, when used inappropriately, will reduce employee engagement, and lead to resistance.

My presence was requested at what I thought was a regular meeting with my director. This meeting was painful, but in hindsight, this was when I truly began living my purpose. I recalled hearing "*Some of your employees are not happy. They do not feel like coming to work in the mornings. They are not committed.*" Wow! Time out! I thought I was doing an amazing job. Things were being accomplished! How could this be?

I remembered sitting in the meeting room and crying non-stop for almost two hours. I was crushed and disappointed; I felt rejected. The thought of failing as a leader was unimaginable. Life threw a curveball I was not prepared to catch. The tears flowed; in that moment of pain, an emotional state of sadness was my only response.

Personal mastery reminds us that in the absence of a shared vision, when each person does not have a personal vision but is enlisted in someone else's vision, you will have compliance but never commitment. The organization had a vision, the project had a vision, I had a personal vision, but the team did not have a shared vision. I did not take the time to speak less and listen more. I did not invest the time to know my team: their hopes, visions, and aspirations. There were no issues with compliance. I had compliance from the head but did not inspire commitment from the heart.

Faced with this unpleasant experience, a battle raged in my mind. The war between my current reality and my vision resulted in creative tension. Creative tension, the force that comes into play when one's vision is at odds with reality, meant my vision was at odds with what was happening. How would I face all my employees after receiving this feedback? To have someone violate your values is a major disruption; but when you violate your own values it is a disaster. What a tangled web was woven, and in those moments my mind was focused on failure.

In *The Fifth Discipline,* Peter Senge shares that "Failure is, simply, a shortfall, evidence of the gap between vision and current reality. Failure is an opportunity for learning—about inaccurate pictures of current realities, about strategies that did not work as expected, about the clarity of vision." I knew all this stuff about personal mastery was true but in that moment, this pill was too big and difficult to swallow. Negative thoughts joined the fight in my mind, predicting doom and gloom. The thoughts of becoming a laughingstock to the consultants were scary. It was getting late and I could not continue to hold my director hostage watching me cry. I will never forget his advice to me: *"Get to know your staff."*

What happened next revealed my character and began shaping the creation of my living leadership legacy. My response to failure had to be appropriate. I had to reach deep into my self-awareness account and make a withdrawal from my psychological assets. I had to focus on having a growth mindset, remaining confident, hopeful, and optimistic. I held creative tension and pulled my reality towards my vision, instead of my vision being pulled towards reality. I intentionally pursued personal and leadership development with key coaches in my corner for accountability. I have often wondered, what would have happened to my destiny if I did not change the inner attitudes of my mind? There was no logical reason to abandon my vision but my goals had to be adjusted.

Driving home without a full understanding of the consequences of this incident, I used the time to reflect on this leadership dilemma and the gaps in my leadership competencies. I was hurting inside, and had to sort through the chaos to understand the invisible force, my emotions, which was infiltrating my mind. My thoughts screamed failure and inexperience, and my emotions were focused on disappointment and sadness.

- **Disappointment:** Words could not express my emotional state of being; I was disheartened and saddened to face the realization that, on a team I valued, some were committed with their heads but not inspired from their hearts. I was disappointed that my team members did not feel connected enough to share their true feelings with me. I was accountable for this result, because as the leader I was responsible for creating an environment conducive to open communication. I was deceived into thinking the group was cohesive, and placed my focus on the tasks that were needed, but did not care enough for the needs of my team.

- **Inexperience:** Though I was passionate and determined, I was a rookie manager who didn't understand the significance of employee engagement, which was my primary source of failure. The employees were producing the deliverables but never beyond what was expected. The inspiration they needed to go above and beyond was absent.

- **Team Failure:** Let's face it: my accountability was to lead the team and organization to success for this initiative. I was entrusted to care for the team and employees' well-being while making the best decisions and serving the purpose of the organization. I was responsible for creating an environment conducive to success, inspiration and empowerment. This was not the team's reality. I had failed the team.

- **Personal Failure:** Introduce me to one person who does not hold the desire to be successful and I will tell them they have stopped living. I had failed on my first major deliverable as a leader. I had failed at people change management. I had failed at employee engagement. I had failed management, who believed in me, and I failed me by violating my own personal values. The evidence of failure surrounded me. How would the driving forces of my emotions shape my response?

How would I overcome the pain and discomfort and get back on track with my vision? One thing is certain: challenging the status quo is never a comfortable place. It's not a popularity contest, neither is it for the faint of heart. I was confident this failure could not define who I am or my potentials. This failure was an opportunity to grow and learn about the inaccurate picture of my perspective of reality. Renewing my mind, getting away from thoughts of failure, and leveraging a growth mindset were necessities for moving towards my vision.

I believe the battle begins in your mind but success begins with your mindset. I was one thought away from either killing my vision or breathing life into my vision. Your thoughts will produce the visions for the dimensions of your life but your mindset will determine if these become achievable. I was committed to the truth and ready to remove any limiting beliefs, increase my self-awareness, and deepen my understanding of leadership.

The actors were all gone and the curtains were closed. The story continued but now there was only one producer, one film crew, one screenwriter, and one actress. I was formally introduced to me at a different stage in this business of life. This called for saying goodbye to the past, which is not my destiny, and hello to a fresh perspective with new insights.

I was committed to continuing to pursue personal mastery and even more committed to personal development. We each produce several stories, but your story will never end until you give permission to close the curtains. This is how powerful you are. There were many lessons to reflect on and new things to learn. This was a time for growing and I valued the opportunity to develop as a world-class leader.

A Growth or Fixed Mindset

"Little minds are tamed and subdued by misfortunes; but great minds rise above them." —Washington Irving

Mindsets play a significant role in all aspects of a person's life. Mindsets create expectations, locking you into a realm of reality that will impact your achievements. In her role as Professor of Psychology at Stanford University, Carol S. Dweck documented the theory of mindset psychological traits. Dweck characterizes individuals who believe their success is based on innate ability as having a fixed mindset. Individuals with growth mindset, on the other hand, attribute their success to hard-work, learning, and training.

Individuals with a fixed mindset hold limiting perspectives towards growth. Challenges are perceived to be negative and not an opportunity for growth. They quit easily in the face of adversity and avoid obstacles because of the fear of failure. People with fixed mindsets believe you will either be successful or not, depending on the way you were wired at birth (DNA). As a result, there is no real reason to go the extra mile and apply effort. They are threatened by the success of others yet they fail to embrace constructive feedback needed for growth.

Individuals with a growth mindset do not create or

nurture space for a quitting zone. They embrace challenges and remain persistent in the face of adversity. They believe repeated effort is needed to develop success, personal mastery, and as a result they thrive on constructive feedback. They learn from the successful lessons of those who have blazed the trails.

I knew my glory as a world-class leader would only come from my source of power, and tapping into my psychological and intellectual assets with a growth mindset. My mind had to be renewed and all evidence of failure filtered to pave the way for me to experience the glory of success. The famous writer Napoleon Hill once said, "The majority of men meet with failure because of their lack of persistence in creating new plans to take the place of those which fail." I was ready to create my new growth plan.

In my leadership challenge, my setback did not equate to a step back but meant an opportunity to "fail forward," with a renewed mind, innovative ways of thinking, new perspectives, and fresh ideas. Renewing the mind is not a one-time activity. It requires lifelong learning. With a completion mindset (a mindset determined to complete what was started) I would not allow roadblocks to persist and become permanent obstacles. There was no space in my mind to be stuck in past unpleasant experiences.

I desired to live an experience of being the best leader of people and organizations. To attain my vision, I made three key decisions. The first decision was to channel my emotions, energy and resources towards the future. Once I understood and accepted the past, I began looking forward. This decision

RE-NEW YOUR MIND

meant releasing the past.

The second decision was to settle in my mind that this situation was not hopeless. There are many valuable life lessons I've learned from my greatest cheerleader and my precious mother, Zeris; one of which is to believe in myself at all times, and my leadership capabilities. I am a leader with the power to design my future. I am a leader who would not allow the emotions of rejection to change my opinion about myself. I am a leader who would not allow the product (me) or service (demonstrated gifts and knowledge) to be misrepresented. A leader who is confident in the characteristics (DNA) that makes up my identity. A leader who perceived failure as an opportunity for course correction, change, and adapting while focusing on the destination. Giving up was not an option; I would continue to move forward and keep my eyes focused on the destination – my purpose. This decision meant developing self-awareness.

The third decision was, the present is here, leverage the current opportunities. The past is behind me, learned from it. Hopelessness was not an option because the future is ahead of me, and I would prepare for it. In the present my vision needed to push forward instead of backwards. This decision meant managing the present.

A new story of transformation was being scripted. The main plot was renewing my mind, breaking patterns of failure and limiting beliefs that could have prevented me from failing forward. The story conflict involved the lead actress having to release the past, develop self-awareness, and manage the present. In releasing the past, I embraced vulnerability and

[41]

resisted the urge to shy away from uncomfortable situations. It became necessary to understand the past and gain hindsight into who, what, why, where and when? I had the most difficult conversations with all my employees, but it was necessary to reach across the lines and connect with them.

Developing self-awareness took me down a path where understanding my emotions, thought process, strengths, values and belief systems and competency gaps were top of mind. I acknowledged the limitations and refused to be stuck. Awareness included gaining insights about the team I was entrusted to lead. One of the most effective advices I received was from my director: *"Get to know your people."* Acting on this advice I gained insight on the fundamental human needs that were missing from the team. A sense of worth was missing and this triggered inferiority, mediocrity and dis-engagement. A sense of belonging was missing which made some team members feel insecure and triggered conflicts. A sense of competence was missing which resulted in some employees settling into unproductive routines. My method was bold and courageous; confronting the challenge and facing my team in humility. I cared about my integrity, and choose to honor my team while remaining an authentic leader.

I managed the present by tapping into the kingdom of education to acquire knowledge. I studied the foundations and concepts of emotional intelligence, situational leadership, and employee engagement strategies. I understood there is a powerful force at play, something much bigger than the universe, and that it was okay to trust, let go, and allow faith in Jesus Christ to be the foundation of my future success.

I prepared for the future by embracing the change in my leadership competencies and behavior. I got into the "power seat" and recognized the level of control I had in shaping the outcomes. I have the power of choice; the power to release the past; the power to renew my mind; the power to act; the power to activate the seeds of potentials within me; the power to re-write old stories of failure with new stories of success, and the power to live my big dream.

The good thing about this story is that the lead actress was resilient, adaptable, and in control of the rules in this game. In this plot, the villains, which were the negative thoughts and status quo, were locked away. Negativity from external forces had no power to silence my voice and passion. The voices of critics and rejection could not influence the way I perceived myself. I remained focused on growing and developing, with a simple slogan: If my heart can conceive it and my mind can believe it then I will achieve it. The renewal of my mind included connecting to my faith, spending time in the presence of great leaders and attending leadership seminars to experience great leaders in action.

I re-programmed my mind to think at a different level. I was strategic about what I allowed my eyes to see, my ears to hear, my heart to believe, and my mouth to speak. Corrupt and negative thoughts were denied access to my mind. I was blessed to have support from great coaches, who played major roles in my personal and leadership transformation. I was transformed into an effective leader, and have since won numerous leadership awards locally and globally, leading myself, others, and organizations.

The outcomes of renewing my mind were beyond my imagination. The entire team became fully engaged, and transitioned into a high-performing team. Despite the setbacks and leadership challenge, we collaboratively implemented the initiative within the committed timelines. The consulting firm (which had initially believed we did not have the necessary competencies) honored me and the team for our outstanding work. I was a stronger leader and gained the reputation of being able to successfully coach low-performing employees into high-performing team members, and build global innovation teams.

Years later, I am still in contact with the members of this team. I have employed some in other organizations and watched others rise into management. If you were to conduct a 360-degree leadership interview with everyone that I've had the pleasure of leading, the unanimous response would be "*She is the best leader we've ever had.*" Businessman Harvey Firestone Jr. said, "The growth and development of people is the highest calling of leadership." I am living my purpose: being the best leader I can be. I have become a living leadership legacy wrapped in people and organizational leadership, discovered through my failures as a rookie manager. I have committed to shifting from the old and embracing the new, and I am now the founder of a leadership consulting practice. Big dreams do come true, but they require decisions, focus, resilience, and commitment.

In pursuit of your vision, renew your mind to see fresh perspectives. Setbacks may require your goals and vision to be

RE-NEW YOUR MIND

changed or updated, but your purpose will not change. As you manage creative tension, keep this in mind—especially when you are envisioning the future. I achieved success because I embraced failure, managed personal change, and developed a passion for learning various leadership approaches. My perspective on failure is that it is, and always will be, an opportunity for unlimited success. The key to personal mastery is the constant renewal of your mind, learning, and insights, which leads to discoveries and drives new actions.

What is your personal offering to the world? What will you contribute? We each have a personal offering the world is waiting for, but these seeds of potential will remain dormant unless you take the responsibility to renew your mind, challenge your status quo and consistently be aware of what's coming next.

Stories of persistence, learning, challenging the status quo, maintaining a growth mindset, and renewing the mind will reveal leaders who have vision, purpose, and personal mastery. Madonna Buder is an exemplary leader who is persistent and pursued personal mastery. On October 5, 2010, Madonna Buder released her autobiography, *The Grace to Race: The Wisdom and Inspiration of the 80-Year-Old World Champion Triathlete Known as the Iron Nun*. Buder sought to improve her mind, body, and spirit and began training at age forty-eight.

At fifty-five Buder completed her first Ironman event. At seventy-five Buder became the oldest woman ever to complete the Hawaii Ironman race. At eighty-one Buder became the world record holder for the Ironman Kona World Championship. In 2012, at eighty-two, Buder competed in the

Ironman triathlon again, and was the oldest person to finish the Subaru Ironman Canada. In 2014, Buder was inducted into the USA Triathlon Hall of Fame.

Buder was successful; however, there were times when Buder had to manage creative tension as her reality contended with her vision. In 2008 at age 79, Buder participated in the Ironman race, but she was unable to reach the finish line by a factor of seconds. In 2009, at age 80, she completed Ironman Canada and broke her own record of being the oldest female to complete the race. However, this was after the Ironman organization extended the age bracket to allow her to compete, because Buder's age was outside Ironman age limit. In 2010, Buder started the Ironman Canada competition at age 80, but withdrew from the race due to a wetsuit issue. It would have been easy for Buder to give up with the setbacks and challenges she encountered, but she persisted, and became the oldest male or female to finish an Ironman triathlon.

Buder's age was not a limitation and had no bearing either on her mind or external orientation. She was committed to the truth by not allowing her age to be a limitation and believed in her ability to create the future she desired. She engaged her mind and emotions to resolve the creative tensions and retired from the triathlon as a world record holder. This is persistence, challenging the status quo, and personal mastery in action.

Five Principles to Renew Your Mind

"The past is behind; learn from it. The future is ahead; prepare for it. The present is here; live it." —Unknown

The process of renewing your mind is a continuous act that requires the right understanding, humility, honour, pure thoughts, the right expression of speech, and going to deeper levels to filter out thoughts contrary to your beliefs and values. From my successful personal experience, here are five recommended principles to help renew your mind.

- **Principle 1:** Master Self-Awareness
- **Principle 2:** Connect with Your Faith
- **Principle 3:** Release the Past
- **Principle 4:** Manage the Present
- **Principle 5:** Think Right Thoughts

Principle 1
Master Self-Awareness

"Mastering others is strength; mastering yourself is true power." – Lao Tzu

Renewing your mind begins with connecting with who you are. Personal (or self-) awareness is the ability to understand your emotions, habits, values, beliefs, and psychological needs. Connecting with your thoughts (including the assumptions, beliefs, perspectives, and interpretations you hold of people, places, and things) drives your past actions, present behaviours, accomplishments, mindset, and establishes your future.

Becoming an influential leader who is responsible for shaping your future cannot be attained without personal awareness. It is the key to building your character, creating strong relationships, and having an authentic presence. A leader who has a powerful sense of personal awareness can readily answer these four questions:

- **Identity:** Who am I?
- **Passion:** What are my desires?
- **Reality:** What's the focus of my thoughts?
- **Purpose:** How am I making a difference?

With a solid understanding of your answers to these questions, you will be empowered to embrace change and make plans for growth and development. Possessing this level of awareness will position you for success. In my rookie leadership challenge, I became aware of my limitations, weaknesses, and the things that threatened me, as well as my strengths, knowledge, and skills. This awareness became the agent of change in the creation of my living leadership legacy. I became attuned to my inner systems: the values and beliefs that guided my actions. I knew how to leverage my strength and had no fear of reaching out for help. Without being self-aware, overcoming the leadership challenge would have been difficult and perhaps impossible. To increase your personal awareness, make a commitment to implement all or some of the actions I continuously use in my business of life.

- Be open-minded and embrace change.

- Get in touch with your beliefs and values systems.
- Clarify your personal vision, goals, and priorities.
- Conduct personal SWOTs to discover dormant potentials.
- Understand your emotional triggers and create default responses.
- Keep a strong focus on your priorities. This will serve you well when roadblocks, setbacks, and adversities present challenges.
- Seek feedback from family and trusted peers who can access your blind spots. They will point out areas of opportunity even if it hurts.
- Practice reflection. Reflect on what you are trying to achieve. What is working well and what needs a different approach?
- Assess if your passion and reality is in alignment with your purpose.
- Be confident in who you are, and refuse to let the voice of cynicism influence your thoughts.

Principle 2
Connect with Your Faith

"What this power is I cannot say; all I know is that it exists and it becomes available only when a man is in that state of mind in which he knows exactly what he wants and is fully determined not to quit until he finds it." —Alexander Graham Bell

Our minds hold viewpoints that must be exposed to truth. Truth is one of the most important concepts in life that will set you free from guilt, shame, deception and play a significant role in decluttering your mind. Your perception of the world and your experiences works from the outside to the inside to influence your mind and thought process. The world is filled with many arguments from multiple sources—the media, the internet—readily available at your fingertips. It is important to understand the various things that are sending signals to your belief system to better control what shape your beliefs and distort the truth. You must be able to distinguish truth from lies, and fact from fiction to appropriately filter out unwanted incoming messages.

Renewing your mind is a process that begins on the inside. This process starts when truth is embraced in humility and you are connected to your source of power and faith. Once connected, you will be guided by the still, small voice that some refer to as intuition. I refer to that still, small voice as Jesus Christ. Your mind, will, and emotions will tap in to your faith to create a powerful connection, paving the way for truth to override lies. When this happens, be quick to recognize self-defeating thoughts, behaviours, and habits, and replace them with who you were created to be—a person with vision, hope, and purpose. Become aware that whatever you think about and focus your thoughts on, you will become. Set your mind to think about things that are good, pure, just, positive, and excellent rather than being consumed by societal norms.

Connecting to your faith is a foundational step in the lifelong process of renewing your mind and achieving your dreams. Faith means your confidence, dependency, trust and reliance on a person, and most significantly faith in Jesus Christ. I remember June 15, 2012 when I sat with my eyes glued to the television watching ABC station broadcast the Nikolas "Nik" Wallenda tight-rope walk over Niagara Falls. This was an unprecedented feat which was banned by both the Canadian and United States Governments for over one hundred and twenty-five years. Wallenda was finally granted permission and became the first person to walk a tight-rope stretched directly over Niagara Falls.

I watched the night closed in on Wallenda and the heavy mist over the Falls, as Wallenda spoke words of encouragement, *"This is what dreams are made of people. Pursue your dreams, never give up. Focus on the other side."* What was more interesting was the deep connection to his faith. As Wallenda walked the tight-rope he repeated, *"Praise you Father God. Praise you Jesus."* Wallenda considered the connection to his faith as a core aspect of his life. He lives with the memories of Wallenda family members who died in acrobatic acts, including his great grandfather who fell to his death during a tight-rope walk in Puerto Rico. Yet, despite the setbacks and tragedies Wallenda never gave up his passion and dreams. He remained committed, passionate, renewed his mind and depended on his faith in God.

Connecting to your faith is vital in the process of renewing your mind. The strong confidence and trust in your faith will help you to replace limiting beliefs with empowering beliefs. Every emotion you experience, and every word you speak begins in your mind and heart. The quality and outcome of your life is a direct result of your thoughts, emotions, actions, and faith connection.

Connection to your faith plays a significant role in transforming unproductive habits. Entrenched unproductive habits will become obstacles that prevent you from achieving your dreams. Unproductive habits are evident in your vocabulary and actions. Speaking words such as "I can't", or including overuse negative qualifiers such as "no" or "but" can be perceived by others that you are right and they are wrong. It can be evident in your behaviour such as throwing your hands in the air, walking away, and quitting at the first sign of a difficult situation. Changing these unproductive habits requires a renewing of the mind.

When your mind is entrenched in unproductive habits Daniel Goleman, the emotional intelligent guru and co-author of *Primal Leadership*, states, "It takes commitment and constant reminders to stay focused on undoing those habits. Over time, the need for reminders will diminish as the new behaviour becomes a stronger pathway in the brain." When you are committed to the process of growth and allow your mind to be renewed, and your thoughts to operate in truth by connecting to your faith, unproductive habits become easier to be transformed.

The good news is, once your mind is renewed you have the power to control the outcome of your business of life. You have the power to think right thoughts and filter out incoming messages that are contrary to the truth. You will get to the state of mind where the connection to your faith enable you to see fresh perspectives, and the impossible becomes possible. Wallenda believed, and the impossible became possible. Today, Wallenda is recognized in the Guinness World Record Book for his accomplishments and spectacular stunts.

A clear mind with positive thoughts and productive habits becomes a fertile ground to envision, plan, create, and execute your desired future.

Principle 3
Release the Past

"When one door closes, another opens; but we often look so long and so regretfully upon the closed door that we do not see the ones which has opened for us." —Alexander Graham Bell

Letting go is never easy. It can be difficult and emotional. Whether the past was filled with disappointments, unhealthy habits, or joyful memories, there comes a time when you must move on. This means understanding the events of the past, listening and learning from these messages, accepting them, and then releasing them. Depending on the person and situation, letting go the past may create a sense of loss or a sense of relief and gratitude. Regardless of the emotional expression and attachment to the past, your past has no power to dictate your future. The only power the past will have is the power you decide to give it. The events that have occurred in the past cannot be changed but you can change your perspective to create the future. Every breath you take presents an opportunity to release the past, and open yourself to a world of new possibilities.

Have you ever wondered why, when the right course of action is known, there is a struggle to follow through? People allow themselves to be stuck in patterns of past experiences instead of leaping at the chance to renew their minds and release the past. The energy and time spent on negative memories will add burdens to your shoulders and weigh you down. Positive memories can have a similar effect. Holding on to pleasant memories can trigger contentment and acceptance of the status quo. You are forever celebrating past accomplishments, and blind to new opportunities that present themselves.

I'm always fascinated by the story of the process eagles go through to regenerate their talons when faced with limited mobility due to aging. Eagles are presented with two options at this point: they wither and die or go through a painful process of change. This change requires the eagle to build a nest on the top of a mountain and remain there until the regeneration process is completed. The eagle then takes flight, soaring in the skies. Leaders are born to soar, not to be burdened with memories. Deep attachment to the past limits the ability to sense, scan, and respond to the future.

Releasing the past will enable you to see with a new perspective. Like the eagle, operate from a higher place. As painful as the process may seem, release the past, and take flight into the present and onto the future. In *Theory U*, Otto reminds us, "In order to rise to the occasion, leaders often have to learn how to operate from the highest possible future, rather than being stuck in the patterns of our past experiences." With an open mind, give yourself permission to appreciate the past and release the past, to live, manage the present, and design the future. The power to write a new story is to decide today to take flight, soar high, and release yesterday's story. There comes a time when you must let go in order to grow. Let that time be right now.

Principle 4
Manage the Present

"The power for creating a better future is contained in the present moment: You create a good future by creating a good present." —Eckhart Tolle

To manage the present, a clear and accurate perspective of the current reality is of paramount importance. This is challenging to achieve if your mind is confused, your vision is cloudy, and you are emotionally unstable. In a world where things are rapidly changing, it is easy for setbacks to trigger feelings of powerlessness. Leaders must take control of their emotions, practice emotional self-management, and manage their imaginations. To manage the present, keep your eyes focus on the destination and not the journey. When the destination is your focus, the bumps, twists, and turns along the way will be easier to navigate.

Manage the present by dispelling disempowering beliefs. Be relentless in discovering, understanding, and removing the factors that blind your eyes to what is and what could be, while living in the present. Be curious in your daily affairs and challenge what you are seeing and hearing to ensure that the right actions to support your vision are being taken.

Always remember that what you see today is tomorrow's old news. What lies in the future may be uncertain and unknown, but aim to live in the present with eyes on the future and know there is always something more, something greater, something new, and something waiting to be discovered. In the present, develop a mindset of anticipation and hope. Having the right mindset and listening to the still, small voice will pave the way to a future filled with revelations, opportunities, and innovations.

As you manage the present, remember you have the power of choice. Make the right choices to support your desired future state while satisfying the present. My decision to pursue a doctorate in education (leadership specialization) was strategic and intentional. I had scanned the horizon and gained foresight into future opportunities, which would require educational research consultants. I took the actions necessary to be ready when this opportunity fully presented itself. I am gaining knowledge in educational research now while preparing for the future.

The more you focus your thoughts on your goals and vision in the present, the more you will bring them into reality in the future. Your beliefs will fuel your thoughts. Your thoughts will drive your emotions and your focus. Your emotions and focus will drive your actions and your actions will determine your outcomes. It is your responsibility to manage the present by keeping your mind renewed and your energy focused on the things that matter most and make a difference.

Principle 5
Think Right Thoughts

"If you truly want to change your life, you must first be willing to change your mind." —Donald Altman

One of the factors that distinguish those who are successful from those who struggle to accomplish their goals is their thoughts. Whatever you plant in your mind will reap a harvest. Seeds of doubt will reap crop failure and seeds of faith will reap a fruitful harvest. Majority of what you see outside yourself reflects the internal thoughts you have focused on all your life. Your thoughts will drive the experiences in your business of life. You cannot allow your thoughts to be focused on past failures or present mistakes because these do not determine your future outcomes. Your future outcomes are determined by the seeds you give life to in your thoughts. Like a gardener tending seeds until they become a flower, the seeds you nurture will eventually grow. These seeds sown into the soil of your mind will eventually burst, bud and produce a harvest. The type of harvest you reap will depend on the kind of seeds you planted in your thoughts, and how they were nurtured.

In this business of life, when you envision the future, what flows outward reflects your internal values, beliefs, knowledge, experiences, and thoughts. To begin renewing your

mind and thinking right thoughts:
- Commit to exchanging negative thoughts for positive thoughts.
- Guard your heart and be selective in who has access to your ears.
- Conduct a self-diagnostic test to check if your incoming and outgoing thoughts are based on truth. Are your thoughts pure or packed with hidden motives? Are they honourable and excellent?
- Understand your emotional triggers and create default responses.
- Be confident in your capabilities and create plans to close any gaps.
- Adopt a growth mindset and believe you have the power to change.
- Allow your source of faith to become the final authority.
- Plant and nurture your seeds with faith.

If your insights from the self-diagnostic test reveal a fixed mindset, give yourself permission to challenge the status quo and form new habits that support a growth mindset. If the test reveals a mindset that sees problems as barriers to success, use your power of choice, and choose to embrace challenges as opportunities. If your desire is to attract the resources needed to help you achieve your vision, you must understand that no one is attracted to a fixed mindset. A fixed mindset will repel potential sponsors; a growth mindset will attract the resources you need to create your future.

Pay attention to your influencers. Create circles of friends who are positive thinkers and stay away from those who are negative thinkers. If your friends do not genuinely celebrate you, turn off the light switch before your thoughts become influenced by negative behaviours. Failure to pay attention to negative influencers will open the door for the law of reproduction to take effect.

George Bernard Shaw an Irish Play writer and critic once said, "Progress is impossible without change, and those who cannot change their minds cannot change anything." Leverage the power of reflection to analyse your thoughts. Reflect on your days—the conversations you participated in, your responses—and observe your emotional state. Commit to thinking right thoughts and filtering out thoughts that will trigger creative tension between the current reality and your vision. Progress and change will only become possible when your mindset is renewed and your thoughts are positive.

Big Dreams Don't Just Happen
Action Plan to Re-New Your Mind

Renewal of the mind is a choice and you hold that power of choice. What you focus your thoughts on, you will achieve and become. As you pursue personal mastery, begin to create default behaviors by affirming the thoughts you want to drive positive results. Below is my partial recommended list of "I will" and "I have" affirmative statements to begin re-programming your mind for growth.

- I will pursue personal (self-) awareness.
- I will choose to nurture a growth mindset.

- I will nurture an open mind and an open heart.
- I will extract value from failures and see opportunities.
- I will be confident in my competencies and capabilities.
- I will be open to interrupting patterns of negative habits.
- I will feed my mind with empowering beliefs and thoughts.
- I will focus in the present moment to make future changes.
- I will think pure, honorable, beautiful, and excellent thoughts.
- I will be open to feedback because this is an opportunity for growth.
- I will see failure as a stepping-stone to success rather than the enemy.
- I will step outside my comfort zone and permit myself to be vulnerable.
- I will recognize that yesterday has ended and does not dictate my future.
- I will watch the relationships I nurture, which can influence my success.
- I will manage creative tension and not be influenced by negative emotions.
- I will create the life I want in all dimensions of my business of life.
- I have the power within me, and the faith to accomplish all things.

CHAPTER FOUR
RE-ENVISION YOUR FUTURE

"If you don't design your own life plan, chances are you'll fall into someone else's plan. And guess what they have planned for you? Not much." —Jim Rohn

For many, mentioning the future may bring frightening thoughts. For others, uncertainty and the unknown bring excitement and hope. If you believe your business of life is not where it should be, here is the opportunity to re-envision your future. A leader without a vision will focus all their energy in the present because tomorrow is perceived as a speck in the distant future. The reality is, if you are not connected to a life plan designed specifically for your life, chances are you're living the agenda of someone else's life plan. You are accountable to create the future you desire and live your vision.

Purpose, vision, and values are foundational in the creation of your growth plan. Clarity must exist for all three. Your purpose answers the "Why?" "Why do you exist?" "How do you contribute to making a difference in the world?"

Many of us go through life wondering and trying to discover

our purpose. We are confident there is a reason for being but unable to connect the dots. Our minds and thoughts are too busy adapting to the experiences of life to become aware of our purpose. Often times our purpose is starring at us but our eyes are closed. We cannot see it. Our hearts are closed. We cannot understand it. Without recognizing our purpose, we are prone to becoming disillusioned. The key to discovering your purpose is to shift your focus inwards rather than seeking outwards to discover the precious gems on the inside that is waiting to reveal your purpose.

What are the dreams of your heart? What drives you to become passionate and take action? Do you carry a burden for others who are in need of care? Does your life serve something of value that transcends beyond your personal gain? To identify your purpose, practice reflection and introspection to awaken the dreams that are lying dormant inside of you.

Your vision will speak to the destination of your future life. It will create a roadmap for success and become a force in the creation of your future. Your vision becomes an expression of your values and an internal compass that guides your lifestyle, decisions, and actions on your journey in this business of life. Designing, creating, or tweaking your vision will not be achieved by doing things the same way you have always done them. It is necessary for leaders to pause, reflect, and challenge the processes and methods used to achieve their vision. See the opportunities for change and embrace the new. As you journey towards your destination watch for dream killers. Be decisive in separating yourself from toxic relationships and negative thinkers who are not in sync with your beliefs and core values.

Your core values will answer the questions "How should I act?" and "Is this behavior consistent with my purpose?" Values describe how your business of life plays out moment by moment as you pursue your vision. The journey to your desired destination should be perceived as running a marathon. How you lead yourself and manage your values, vision and purpose during the marathon will determine if you arrive at the destination.

Leadership begins on the inside and reflects on the outside. Leadership is required to achieve your passion which is expressed in your vision statement and connects with your purpose. No leadership. No passion. No purpose. Everyone should be intentional about creating a life plan. The formulation of your plan begins in your heart and mind. If you live in the present without a plan, expect the future to arrive and leave you in the past. I promised myself that in the later years of my life I will look back and have no regrets. I will see a life filled with purpose, vision fulfilled, and a living leadership legacy. My purpose is expressed as "Being the best leader I can be."

There was a period in my life when I lived the vision of someone else's plan. Reflecting on this period, I had no plans for children, community service, establishing strong relationships, or living a healthy lifestyle. I considered my first degree sufficient. My plan was to execute the plan of someone else until the truth of Jesus Christ came, and my mind was renewed. I started seeing with an open mind and an open heart. Now I am intentionally managing my business of life in the present and envisioning the future. There's a plan for every dimension of my life, and I hold myself accountable for creating and executing the goals that will realize my vision.

My first degree, in commerce (business and information systems), included developing business solutions using Hypertext Markup Language (HTML) programming. During those years, having knowledge of HTML was cool, popular and sufficient to create a fully functioning website. Having this knowledge satisfied my vision of becoming a software developer and served my purpose. Years later, as I've moved into a leadership position, the industry has changed and HTML is no longer a key programming language. There is now a suite of new languages and specifications that changes rapidly: EJB (Enterprise Java Beans), Java, JavaServer Faces (JSF), and Struts, to name a few. HTML is still being used but it cannot satisfy all the demands of the technology revolution and consumer needs for digital solutions.

What would have happened had I chosen not to challenge my status quo and continued learning? What would have happened to my business of life had I decided not to release the successful memories of using HTML? What if I had not renewed my mindset and freed myself to learn and adapt to new languages and new ways of software development?

This business of life is no longer business as usual; it is not static and external factors will force change. In *Primal Leadership* the authors shared that, "Visions change, but as the vision evolves, the leader needs to be sure that the 'sacred centre'—what everyone hold paramount—remains intact." Your vision may not unfold perfectly as designed; this is okay because your purpose is the foundation of the vision and that remains consistent. Embracing change is necessary to deal with the bumps, twists, and turns of life, and to bring the future into the present. Going through your business of life without re-envisioning your goals and plans would not serve your purpose. The rapid changes will force you to exit the growth and development process making you irrelevant.

Digital transformation, globalization, and social connectedness challenge old patterns, old ways of thinking, and the status quo. I could not settle for only a first degree because the digital age demands a new kind of leadership with specific competencies. I was faced with the decision to challenge my status quo and re-envision my future to create the new 21st century leadership style. In pursuit of personal mastery, and moving with the ebb and flow of the digital age, I completed my master of arts (in leadership) degree. This required an updated vision statement and new goals, which came with twists and turns. However, in pursuit of personal mastery, I held creative tension and managed my emotions.

When I was completing the last four months of the master's program, I became ill and needed major surgery, which required four to six months of recovery. I was in the middle of finishing my capstone project when my vision became at odds with my current reality. Creative tension set in. I thank my academic supervisor, who was very kind and patient during that time, and the school, which approved an extension. I remembered, while working with my supervisor over the phone, I cried once because of physical pain. The choices were to cave in to the emotional tension and allow my current reality to pull my vision towards it or to hold creative tension and pull the current reality towards my vision. The future does not wait, and I chose to take the necessary actions to bring my current reality in line with my vision.

With persistence, resilience, and determination, I completed my capstone project a month after the deadline, without utilizing the full extension granted. This was not a time to re-envision but a time to hold steady to my vision and manage the setbacks, twists, and turns, because my future depended upon my success in the present. I thank Jesus Christ for His sustaining power. Leaders who are committed to personal growth and mastery don't give up. They adapt and create. There are seven core learnings from my personal experience:

- In this business of life, create and execute the desired vision for your future to ensure you do not live the vision of someone else.
- Constantly review and assess your vision to ensure it is still relevant. Re-envision and update your plans based on current revelations.
- Challenge the status quo. Challenge standard methodologies.
- There will always be a source of creative energy or gaps that stand between your vision and current reality. If this vision is relevant, pull reality towards it. If the vision is no longer relevant, it is okay to stop rather than use your resources to go down the wrong path.
- In this digital age characterized by rapid change, your goals must be current and relevant. Don't become stuck

by being attached to goals that have become irrelevant. Reflect. Review. Release.
- Leaders need to be resilient, adaptive, creative, agile, and futuristic.
- Nurture the perspective that learning is a lifelong process.

Through the process of re-envisioning, your vision and goals must be refreshed to remain relevant. Providing there are cycles of constant monitoring and tweaking of goals, processes, and methods, this process has the potential to yield transformation.

The digital age is changing everything and will continue to use technology to revolutionize the "norms" of humanity. The normal way we bank has changed. We can now bank using the convenience of our smart devices. The way we shop for groceries and clothing has change. We can shop at the mall or shop online. We are encountering a visual overload with images and individual experiences are being tied to an image. The culture of communication has changed. Today global communities are found in chat rooms, on social media and online forums sharing stories, visual contents without filters. The way we see ourselves is being subtly impacted. Your mind becomes a playground impacting your sense of identity by using avatars to express who you are. The way you make friends and the type of friends is changing. The apps on smart devices will now send you an alert when people who share your interest are detected. The ability to connect to these suggested friends are easy, and for those who are shy this would seem perfect. Your intellectual memory is now being outsourced to the cloud. I call this phenomenon "Personal Intellectual Outsourcing." Humans are not dependent on their memory to store information such as phone numbers, addresses or quotes. Our memory is being outsourced to machines in the clouds and robots. There is a new world being formed and it is called the Cyber World, a virtual world in cyber space where information is stored and retrieved. This is a world where we have become active participants without full knowledge of its operation.

The entrepreneurial spirit is on the rise and companies are beginning to create cultures that nurture visionaries to drive innovation. As an example of this process in action, I brought together a group and intentionally took fifteen minutes to teach them an approach to innovation. Three hours later, they were engaged in conducting a design-thinking session, which I facilitated. The group members were coached to be visionaries, and as a result they innovated and prototyped digital solutions for the identified business problems. This is the future: collaboration, creativity, innovation, and agility. Social media platforms continue to transform the way we connect, forging more collaboration. We live in a connected and instant global community. Diverse cultures are being integrated, sharing, and becoming powerful voices of change. It is just not business as usual.

The process of re-envisioning depends on leaders having a vibrant and clear picture of their vision. However, many people are not clear about their vision immediately and may need a time of reflection to appreciate "what was" (the past), "what is" (the present), and to envision "what is to come" (the future). Leaders without a personal vision statement should go through the envisioning process. Leaders who are currently executing against a personal vision will need to go through the re-envisioning process. Here are the four core actions that must be included in updating your growth plan:

- **Action 1:** Reflect on Past Reality
- **Action 2:** Understand Present Reality
- **Action 3:** Sense and Scan the Future
- **Action 4:** Design Your Future

Action 1
Reflect on Past Reality

"To raise new questions, new possibilities, to regard old problems from a new angle, requires creative imagination and marks real advance in science." —Albert Einstein

Reflection is a learning tool that enables leaders to make meaning and learn from their past experiences. Reflecting on past realities enables you to compare expected versus actual outcomes, assess, and address the gaps. An analogy for this concept is a budgeting process. A monthly budget is planned, and at the end of the month, the planned budget is compared with the actual expenditures. The accountant will close the month by identifying and reconciling any gaps and ensuring all appropriate corrective actions are taken.

When you reflect on past realities, you rewind and play back the events that occurred second by second. The realities of your life plan will reveal setbacks, accomplishments, and the methodologies behind them. The intent is to gain hindsight of what happened during these events. Hindsight brings understanding to the factors that contributed to your success, the nature of the people engaged in the event, the processes used, and an assessment of your performance. When harmony exists between your motivation and satisfaction, the course of action is the celebration of your personal growth. Jim Rohn, an author and motivational speaker expressed, "At the end of each day, you should play back the tapes of your performance. The results should either applaud you or prod you." If harmony does not exist, this is the time to become uncomfortable and make changes.

A time of reflection is used to affirm the strengths that contributed to past success and to see which are still relevant in a world of new possibilities. You will gain insights about which strategies contributed to the peaks of success. This level of reflection will equip you to explore new possibilities, and prevent premature judgements and hasty decision-making. Reflection should include past failures because these are learning opportunities. Extract the valuable lessons from setbacks to determine improvement strategies and to ensure past mistakes are not repeated in the future.

Reflecting on the negatives and positives of the past will confirm what really matters to you. Using questions as a technique is powerful. Questions will help you to understand past realities and begin the process of discovering new possibilities. They will draw out what should matter to you, what really matters, and what do not matter. You may be thinking,

"But I already know this." But now you are looking at these elements from a new perspective while taking into consideration internal and external factors, with a futuristic mindset.

Consider the use of fitness monitors. They are developed to help users achieve exercise and food goals to attain their vision of health. They are designed to help people live a healthy lifestyle. These monitors track heart rates, count daily steps, and measure sleep patterns. Patterns are generated and presented as statistics to provide meaningful data for insight and actions. If the stats show slow progress, adjustments can be made to the goals to change the outcomes. The daily allowed calorie count may be lowered and the time spent in the gym may be increased. When there is clarity about what matters, adjustment to the vision statement are allowed, including a new vision (for example, switching to a vegetarian lifestyle).

The principles of creative tension do not include adjusting the vision as a means of corrective action; however, this has changed with the digital age and adjustments are sometimes necessary, provided the purpose remains the same. Emerging patterns can drive changes in goals and visions. In this case, the vision was updated to include adopting a vegetarian lifestyle and the purpose (to live a healthy lifestyle) remained. Reflection takes you on a journey to look inward and backward (hindsight) in preparation for looking outward and forward (foresight) into the future. Hindsight must take place in preparation for foresight.

Action 2
Understand Present Reality

"A dream is your creative vision for your life in the future. You must break out of your current comfort zone and become comfortable with the unfamiliar and unknown." –Dennis Waitley

Unforeseen factors that will impact your vision are always at play. This may result in a change in direction and plans. It will cause you to leave behind familiar things and people to embrace the new. To get to your desired future state, it is necessary to extract opportunities and understanding from the present reality. To re-envision and take the present reality into consideration, there are key activities that must be repeated. A mindset that nurtures lifelong learning must be in place for success to be sustainable. Here are three recommended techniques for understanding present realities:

- Ask Thought-Provoking Questions
- Evaluate Your Goals
- Challenge Your Current Methodologies

Ask Thought-Provoking Questions

"Learning without thought is labor lost; thought without learning is perilous." —Confucius

Begin to understand your present reality by asking thought-provoking questions. Clarify your purpose to solidify your understanding of the basis of your existence and who you were created to be. Checking the clarity of your purpose will bring the present into perspective. You will understand everything that is demanding your time, skills, talents, energy, and financial resources. This is important because purpose is the energy behind your vision.

Responses from the questions should lead back to the "Why?" of your vision. If your vision is to start your own business, then ask yourself: What are my strengths? What am I passionate about? What type of business do I desire and what will be the organizational structure? What are the messages from the stories in my current reality? What would I need to eliminate from these stories to create a new story and a new path? How will I hold clear and true perspectives when things get challenging? Will I cave in under pressure when purchases and expenses are higher than projected income and sales? These thought-provoking questions will reveal deep insights, increase your awareness, and prepare you to take actions leading you towards your vision.

Evaluate Your Goals

"It does not matter where you are coming from, all that matters is where you are going." —Brian Tracy

There comes a moment when the specific, measurable, attainable, realistic, and time-based (SMART) goals you created to support your vision must go through a relevancy test. To begin the relevancy test, generate a list of your current goals. Which goals were successfully completed? Celebrate them! What methodologies were used to achieve success? Understand them! Which goals are still sitting in your in-progress bucket (there is a struggle to get them to the finish line)? Analyze them! Seek to understand the issues and evaluate if the rules and environment under which these goals were created have changed. Which goals are sitting in the to-be-started bucket? Mark them for deletion! It is that simple. There is no time for settling into unproductive routines. If you are waiting to start or complete something new, it must pass a relevancy test.

In a complex and rapidly changing world, your life plans cannot sit around and wait without being impacted. Thirteen years ago, I had big dreams with the big goal of establishing a desktop publishing company. My vision was to become the desktop publishing company of choice. As with any new business venture, time and finances were invested. Three years after start-up, I decided to close the company. When I evaluated the strategic goals, the in-progress and pending goals were no longer relevant. The technology landscape had changed and desktop publishing capabilities were being introduced in many software packages, giving rise to the DIY revolution.

The current reality had pulled my vision towards it. This was because the emerging technological landscape indicated bigger changes were coming. There was no point pursuing a dead end. To get a solid understanding of present reality, assess your goals within the context of social networks, globalization, politics, economics, and digital transformation, among other change factors. Be open-minded, capture the learning opportunities and be quick to make the necessary changes.

Challenge Your Current Methodologies

"As to methods there may be a million and then some, but principles are few. The man who grasps principles can successfully select his own methods." —Ralph Waldo Emerson

You cannot evaluate your goals in isolation. The methodologies used to execute and accomplish the goals must be challenged. In change management initiatives, you may hear the old cliché "If it's not broke, don't fix it." However, for goals to be met and growth to be experienced, leaders must challenge the methodology used to accomplish their goals. Bob Johansen, author of *Leaders Make the Future*, defined the world as the VUCA world. Johansen advised, "Leaders must learn to listen through the noise of a VUCA World of Volatility, Uncertainty, Complexity and Ambiguity." In the VUCA World, processes and methods that worked in the past may no longer work in the present or future. Leaders must practice reflective journaling, listen to the future, and plan for emerging patterns and trends. Insights from listening to the future will help determine the relevancy of the methodologies used in attaining your vision.

Over the past seventeen years, I've experienced the introduction of new software development processes. I started with the waterfall methodology, moved to Rational Unified Process, incorporated the Unified Modeling Language, and now several years later Agile methodology is being used. These methodologies serve the same purpose: software development, but each differs in approach.

Waterfall, as the name suggests, approaches development deliverables sequentially. Waterfall methodology is still being used but volatile changes in technology demand speed of delivery. Competition between businesses drives speed and agility—who will get the next innovative products and services into the hands of the customer? While Waterfall is still being used, this methodology is not nimble. Agile is faster and is executed in smaller sprints, reducing the time to market for products and services. Agile changes the model from customers being engaged at the end of the process to customers being engaged at the start of the process. It is not business as usual!

Challenging an existing methodology requires you to listen and be observant. The observation provides insight into the events taking place in the present. To challenge a methodology, create a map to chart the peaks and valleys in your business of life. How did you attain the peaks? In the valleys, what processes and strategies did you use to get back to peak performance? What patterns and themes can you detect from the map? What remarkable events were taking place and how did these impact your goals during the peaks and the valleys? Understanding the peaks and valleys provides insight into methodologies that no longer work, and the psychological and intellectual assets you leveraged to attain success. This will result in enhanced self-awareness.

Leaders must be willing to challenge the methods used to achieve their goals. With a curious mind, they should inquire how the future is changing. What are employers looking for? What are the latest trends in technology? Then create a strategy to position yourself to remain relevant.

Action 3
Sense and Scan the Future

Change is the law of life. And those who look only to the past or present are certain to miss the future." — John F. Kennedy

When you sense and scan the future, the latest trends, patterns, and opportunities will emerge. There is no room for being stuck in the past or present with the status quo, holding on to goals and visions that are irrelevant. There is no time to be overwhelmed by present events or to fix your eyes on the obvious. This will prevent you from sensing and scanning for the future. As Johansen says, "You cannot listen to the future if you are deafened by the present or stuck in the past. Signals from the future are already here, all around us." Leaders must release the past and renew their minds to hear messages coming from the future clearly. As leaders' shape and create their future, listening to the pulse of the future must become their new norm.

By their very nature, visions are future-oriented and should not be created and forgotten. Leaders must practice scanning and sensing the future for emerging technologies, political, economic and social changes, to understand the impacts on their business of life. Author and contributor to the *Chicken Soup for the Soul* series Alan Cohen says, "To grow, you must be willing to let your present and future be totally unlike your past. Your history is not your destiny." To grow, change must become a part of your vocabulary, and influenced by future activities.

Sensing the future, which is foresight, will trigger insights and pave the way for creativity and innovation in the present. Emerging patterns and themes will serve as inspiration to do things differently in the present as you prepare for the future. Decisions made in the present will change based on what you anticipate might happen in the future. This is the insight leaders need to challenge the status quo, re-new their mind, re-envision their future, and re-define their goals. Johansen explains that the "VUCA World is not unyielding" but "leaders will need to have Vision, Understanding, Clarity and Agility." Perhaps if the many organizations no longer in business or the leaders that find themselves behind, being passed over for promotions, had engaged the use of foresight, then:

- Volatility would have yielded to Vision.
- Uncertainty would have yielded to Understanding.
- Complexity would have yielded to Clarity.
- Ambiguity would have yielded to Agility.

Clarity requires awareness, which is needed to usher in change. Reflection and introspection are important in clarifying what is most important to you. If you want to get to your ultimate purpose, your head cannot be buried in the sand while the world is changing, and constantly emitting signals, around you. Clarity means you will sift through the chaos to determine the right actions to prevent the future from taking you by surprise. Like boiling the frog, failure to scan the environment, analyze data patterns, and observe emerging trends will cause the future to take you by surprise and leave you in the past.

Gaining clarity in the complex world requires flexibility. This means leaders will be clear about their goal and status, and remain open to changing their methods of execution at any time. As you create a plan for your vision and listen to the future, be prepared to be agile in implementing changes.

Action 4
Design Your Future

"All successful people, men and women, are big dreamers. They imagine what their future could be, ideal in every respect, and then they work every day toward their distant vision, that goal or purpose." —Brian Tracy

Creating a vision that resonates with your purpose and values will attract and generate the power, passion, commitment, and resources needed to make it a reality. As you reflect on your current vision statement (or create one), the learning outcomes from the activities that provided hindsight, insight, and foresight will reveal fresh opportunities, and areas that require your attention, to change, update, or create the new vision for your future. Your vision may have already been attained, but this is not the end. Your vision may no longer be relevant, but there are new opportunities waiting. Your vision may still be in progress; now you can tweak it with updated future possibilities. Your purpose will keep the flames burning and the vision will keep the purpose alive.

Peter Senge reminds us, "After the vision has been achieved, it is your sense of purpose that draws you further, that compels you to set a new vision." Senge goes on to share, "This is the reason personal mastery must be a discipline, because it is a process that keeps you focusing and refocusing on what you truly want, on one's vision." As you refocus on your personal vision statement and envision or re-envision the future, the dimensions below are core areas you should consider for inclusion. The dimension of faith is listed first, as this is the driving force behind all other dimensions. Once you are connected to your faith, what you believe in becomes a force that guides all other dimensions.

- Faith
- Health
- Family
- Wealth
- Personal Growth
- Education/Career
- Relationships
- Business
- Community
- Leadership Growth

Your well-crafted vision statements are short phrases that convey your plans and hopes for the future. Every vision statement will have certain characteristics:

- **Destination:** Speak to where you are heading and why?

- **Aspirations:** Indicate what you hope to achieve.
- **Inspirations:** Provide mental stimulation and engages others.
- **Clarity:** Understandable and easy to communicate.
- **Priorities:** Provide focus for your business of life.
- **Boundaries:** Define what you will and will not do or allow.

How do you get there? Start right where you are and rethink the status quo, renew your mind, and sense and scan the future before creating your goals. Are you ready? Here's a quick five-step approach:

Step 1: Clarify Your Purpose and Identify Core Dimensions

Everything begins in the mind; give yourself permission to dream and think big. Jessica Cox and Madonna Buder had big dreams and big goals, which they achieved. You can too. Do not be afraid to step out and bring the opportunities of the future into the present. Begin by using reflective journaling to record the thoughts that come to your mind. Have faith and connect with the still, small voice for guidance. Trust the process and dig deep to understand what is significant to your business of life. Determine the dimensions you will include in your vision statement by asking yourself the following questions:

- Who am I?
- What is my purpose?

- What are my desires for spiritual growth?
- What things do I believe in and seek to demonstrate in these dimensions?
- What are my innate gifts and strengths?
- Who are the people in my life?
- What relationships do I have in my life?
- What are the qualities of those relationships?
- Who do I work with and what do I value most about them?
- What have I accomplished in my career and desire to continue?
- What activities would bring me optimal satisfaction and matter the most?
- How can I give back to the community?
- What leisure pursuits do I enjoy?
- What does my career look like?
- What am I passionate about?
- If I had access to unlimited resources, how would I live my life?
- What satisfying personal leadership qualities have I developed?
- What are my desires for my personal and leadership growth?
- What is my perfect state of being at this moment?
- How will emerging trends and patterns impact these dimensions?

Step 2: Determine Your Values

Values are fundamental in your business of life. Values have a considerable influence on your behavior and attitude. It motivates you and serves as a guide in the decision-making process. Your values will naturally be reflected in your vision statement, but it is important to understand what they are. Create a list of the values that are significant to you by reflecting on the things you cherish. <u>Identify ten core values that resonate with you and would represent your character.</u>

Step 3: Design "What Should Be" (the Future)

Based on your responses in the previous steps, brainstorm and determine the contributions you would like to make to each dimension. How will you contribute to your faith, family, personal growth, relationship or community and all the other dimensions? Ask yourself "Why do I want to do this? Will this get to the heart of what is fundamentally important to me? Does this reflect my identity, passion and purpose? How will this practically influence and change my world?" The information acquired from the hindsight, insight and foresight activities in step 1 is critical and must be applied in this step. Challenge what you have designed as the desired future, and put it through a relevancy test. Is this relevant and needed in the digital age? If necessary, restart and make revisions. It is okay to restart because if the vision is not relevant, it will not have life or gain momentum.

Step 4: Establish Time Frames

Consider a realistic time frame in which the things you desire, "what should be," will manifest. State the time frame within short periods where possible. Remember, your vision requires focus, and it can be refocused depending on the circumstances. If defining the time frame is challenging, pause, reflect, and gather new personal awareness and insights to understand why setting the time frame is difficult.

Step 5: Create a Summary Statement

Write a summary statement for each dimension using present tense, concise statements, and descriptive language. Focus on where you want to go and where you currently are. The foundation of personal mastery is your personal vision and commitment to the truth. Your personal vision usually exceeds your natural power and capabilities but you must believe in what you have envisioned. You must be able to visualize it in the present or initial state before it is accomplished. Complete this process by sharing your summary statement with someone else to create accountability.

Big Dreams Don't Just Happen
Action Plan to Re-Envision Your Life

The business of life does not happen by the process of osmosis. Actions must be informed and intentional. Create the time and space to reflect on your daily activities. For each dimension of your life, keep track of your achievements. Develop and ask yourself powerful questions to dig deeper into understanding the root of any issues. These are questions such as:

- Am I making the most of the present?
- What strategies am I using to manage the present?
- What strategies will I use to listen to, sense, and scan the future?
- Am I leveraging past experiences to understand patterns?
- Am I curious and open-minded in seeing new perspectives?
- Are my hopes, dreams, and aspirations aligned with my purpose?
- What symbols and metaphors represent the present and future me?
- What will I do differently to get there on time and ahead?
- In my business of life, what's the next big dream?

Creative Tension Practice Exercise:

1. Ask yourself, "What do I want to create (vision)?"
2. Reflect, to understand your current reality based on your vision (reality).
3. Compare your vision and current reality to identify gaps. The gaps are the creative tension. What strategies are in place to close these gaps?
4. What changes need to occur to pull the current reality towards your vision?

CHAPTER FIVE
RE-DEFINE YOUR GOALS

"The first step towards success is taken when you refuse to be captive of the environment you first find yourself in." —Mark Caine

Leaders need to have a clearly defined vision, and channel their resources towards its achievement. Goals must be created, and a course charted towards the destination specified in their vision. The timelines for some goals are established based on major milestones, such as birthdays and New Year's Eve. Regardless of when they are established, many of these goals never seem to materialize. The business of life is continuous, and along the journey obstacles may gain access to the course. Sadly, most people lacking resilience will give up.

Obstacles are not the issue; what's lacking is clarity of vision, commitment to the truth, ability to recognize patterns and trends, accountability, and a commitment to personal growth. This is fundamental to gaining personal mastery.

A captain preparing to set sail will chart the course he plans to take towards a specified destination. He has all the components of a SMART goal in place. These goals are:

- **Specific:** Clarity on what will be accomplished in each dimension is included in the vision. The goals are clear, concise, and identify who is engaged, where will this take place, and why it is being done.

- **Measurable:** The key performance indicators and success criteria are established. The methodology for evaluation is defined.

- **Achievable:** The goal can reasonably be accomplished within defined standards of excellence.

- **Realistic:** The ability to influence each goal is understood. Goals are relevant based on emerging trends, and potential setbacks are taken into consideration.

- **Time-Bound:** There are defined start and end dates for when each goal will be achieved.

As the captain and crew sail along, they consistently monitor the climatic conditions to detect changes in the weather. They are engaged in foresight activities to gain insights about the future weather conditions, and to manage changes in the present. They monitor external factors that may influence the attainment of their goals and ultimate vision. The captain will conduct regular check-ins to the port of call, and listen to weather-monitoring stations for additional information. They are intentionally engaged in sensing the future to see what could possibly emerge, and take them off course or force an adjustment to their goals.

When faced with a setback in the form of gusty winds, a storm or hurricane, the captain will need to make an adjustment. The captain may choose to sail around the storm or skip a port. The captain cannot be engaged in emotional meltdowns because the security of many lives is in his hands. His mind must remain focused on the destination. The captain will take new actions, and may add additional goals to keep the ship, crew, and passengers' safe. He is managing creative tension because his vision is at odds with the current reality. Establishing and managing your goals works in a similar manner. You have clarity of destination, goals are set, and adjustments are made along the way to manage creative tension.

The challenge for most leaders is two-fold. First, how do they get started? Second, how do they adjust their goals to leverage insights and foresight, and to tap into new opportunities?

In the VUCA world, establishing goals call for an innovative approach and a change in mindset. Instead of focusing on just setting goals, change your mindset to include identifying the desired experience and growth. The holistic approach will now include integrating your goals, with the personal experience and growth that will result from executing the goals. Goals focus on a specified destination; once the destination is reached, the goal reaches the end of its life. Growth, on the other hand, refers to a lifelong journey that arrives at many ports of call, each creating a new experience. Goals are inspirational and motivate the attainment of your vision, but growth will continuously increase personal development. A goal represents a potential opportunity that is sought after and to be accomplished. Growth is a series of changes and victories, which, over time, become a series of transformational experiences.

You were born with unlimited seeds of potential. A goal will utilize some of your seeds of potential. Growth will consistently tap into your unused seeds of potential, and foster the discovery of hidden potentials. There is no ending to personal growth and experiences. This is a lifelong process.

Personal mastery is a commitment to personal growth and learning. This is where a leader remains committed to consistent growth and is purposeful about growing and realizing untapped potentials.

As you create the growth goals to support your vision, be aware of how they will contribute to your personal growth and unleash your potential. Shift your focus to creating goals that are measured by personal growth. Author and Personal Development Coach Zig Ziglar express this idea when he stated, "What you get by achieving your goals is not as important as what you become by achieving your goals." When your focus is not only centered on the goals that support your vision but is intertwined with your personal experience and growth, the end results are guaranteed to take you closer to achieving a higher level of personal mastery and living your purpose. The **6 Steps Growth Goal Model**™ below was designed to integrate goals, personal experience and growth as you create your goals.

Step 1: Clarity of Vision

Clarifying your vision is the first step in achieving your desired future. Whether you are envisioning, or re-envisioning, you must be clear about what you want to accomplish. Be clear about the experiences you want to live, and let those experiences and growth goals be the fuel that drives your envisioning and re-envisioning. Your vision must be clear, compelling, and communicated to attract the necessary resources. Clarity of vision will require strong personal commitment, a willingness to challenge established theories, and the ability to learn and question intentions.

Step 2: Clarity of Growth Goals

For each dimension included in your vision statement, identify the top five growth goals. Goals serve as an indication you are making progress towards your vision. The absence of goals to support your vision will result in the loss of focus. Identify the value proposition for each goal. Be clear: How will these goals and the corresponding activities enhance personal growth? What personal changes do you expect to experience when the goal is achieved? The value proposition will motivate you, boost your confidence and increase the possibility of success.

A common mistake made during planning is creating SMART goals but failing to develop supporting action plans. Big demanding goals do not have to be perceived as daunting tasks. Apply the process of chunking. Break down each growth goal into bite-size chunks for easy management and articulate the expected outcomes. I will never forget the advice from my business coach as I embarked upon writing this book. My coach said, *"For every goal you want to experience, be intentional and state the expected outcomes."* Incremental chunks executed individually will sum up to equal the big demanding goal.

Step 3: Clarity of Priorities

Managing your priorities requires you to have clarity about where you will spend your energy, what you will focus on, and how you will manage your time. Your dream may be ignited by your passion but this is not adequate to sustain the journey to the destination. Many passionate leaders fail to establish the priorities after the goals are defined and lose their vision.

What strategies will you use to prioritize your time to remain focus to the top growth goals? How will you ensure time is allocated to your top priorities rather than less important activities? There are twenty-four hours in a day; how will you focus your energy? How will you remove distractions? How will a great idea, which appears to be a good thing to do but is unrelated to your ultimate vision, be managed? Will you shift your focus to engage in this new idea? Will you step back to determine the validity of the idea in relation to your goals and priorities? These are some of the daily questions I ask myself to ensure I remain focus.

Be clear on the priority of the top 5 growth goals. The Pareto Principle (also known as the **80/20 rule,** the law of the vital few, or the principle of factor sparsity) suggested by management consultant Joseph M. Juran and named after Italian economists Vilfredo Pareto specifies an unequal relationship between inputs and outputs. The principle interpreted means 20 percent of your invested input which are your priorities is responsible for 80 percent of the results (output) providing your time, energy and resources is spent on the top 20 percent of your priorities.

Utilize the Pareto Principle to guide your priorities in the business of life. Assess new opportunities through the lens of your vision and priorities. Focus on those opportunities that align with existing priorities, and will advance and keep the vision relevant.

Clarifying priorities will keep you focused and ensure you are progressing towards the desired experience. It will serve as an integrity check to ensure you are living your plan versus executing the plan of someone else. It will keep you on the right path towards your destination.

Step 4: Clarity of Methodologies

One of the critical steps in the model is the execution of the growth goals. What processes and procedures will be used to achieve the growth goals? How will you leverage social technology to help you achieve your goals? Your methodology must include joining safe circles with dedicated time to leverage sharing and peer coaching. Become involved in innovation networks to foster a continuous flow of creativity. What mechanisms are built in to challenge the process and the status quo during execution? How will you determine milestones, establish and measure key performance indicators? How will accomplishments be celebrated? How will you handle setbacks and overcome creative tension?

Step 5: Clarity of Relevancy

In the VUCA world, growth goals must be assessed for relevancy. Things may be progressing well, but what's changing? Is the atmosphere in which the growth goals are being executed conducive to growth? Are there pauses to reflect on the processes and current reality to see if they are outdated? How will you assess your growth goals to determine if your goals are relevant to your vision and personal growth? In addition, who are the coaches and mentors providing you with guidance? Are they attuned to the future events? Do they sense and scan the future to detect emerging patterns and trends? Leaders must set aside the time to review where they are, their progress, and identify what needs changing or updating.

Leaders must ensure they conduct environmental scans to identify social, economic, and technological trends that will influence the outcomes of their plans. There are several strategies that leaders may use to listen to the future. These strategies include digital media monitoring, professional and business networks, and subscriptions to magazines or online forums that forecast future emerging trends. A plan that identifies the goals, priorities, processes, and procedures necessary to achieve your vision is excellent but without a strategy to stay in the present and reach into the future for foresight, you run the risk of becoming a prime target for extinction.

Step 6: Put it Out There! See Your Reality!

Accountability is important. It allows others to support you and creates an environment where you are forced to act on your goals. Share your goals with a trusted circle of friends. Start a blog to record the journey, use your coach and mentor to help hold you to what you said you would complete. If you desire personal mastery, self-awareness is the first step. You have unlimited potential locked up inside of you, waiting to be unleashed. Your dreams are waiting to be activated, waiting for you to reach into the future and bring them into the present, waiting for you to become all you were created to be. Begin by challenging your status quo and saying goodbye to comfort zones. Renew your mind, release the disappointments of the past, and begin to embrace the present. Manage the present and live in the moment while preparing for the future.

Big Dreams Don't Just Happen
Action Plan to Re-Define Your Goals

Goals are short-lived and will get you to a certain point. Commit to achieving personal mastery. Commit to creating a growth plan that will take you beyond the short term and into a place of lifelong growth to maximize your potentials. Ask yourself these questions to gain fresh insights as you re-define or establish your goals.

- What is the why behind your goals? How will this show up in your experience?
- What emotions will you create that will allow you to remain focused?
- How will you prioritize your time to focus on what matters most?
- How will you get to a place where you are proactive versus reactive?
- Are your growth goals tangible, relevant, and manageable?
- Your focus attracts energy. How will you plan and utilize your day?
- What methods (procedures) will you use to manage your time?
- Who are the coaches and mentors providing guidance?
- Are your growth goals created based on your strengths?
- Are you flexible in preparing for the future?
- Is there alignment between your vision, purpose, and

growth goals?
- What strategies do you have in place to listen to the future and manage your business of life?

CHAPTER SIX
LEAD FROM THE FUTURE

"For businesses today, it is disruption of the digital kind that is creating the greatest upheaval. Across every industry, boundaries are being torn down as hyperconnected technology redefines the limits of what is possible." —Duncan Tait

Why do you need to lead from the future? How do you prepare yourself to lead from a future that is volatile, uncertain, complex, and ambiguous? Challenging your status quo, renewing your mind, re-envisioning your future, and re-defining your growth goals are significant steps in the right direction. However, although this marks a major milestone in your business of life, you have only just begun. We are living in an age marked by disruption, ever-increasing complexities, ambiguities, and constant change. Leading from the future means paying attention to an ongoing flow of discoveries, innovation, and transformation, with no stones left unturned. Future-oriented thinking must become part of your core value system. Leading from the future requires a new set of leadership competencies. The traditional leadership competencies that facilitated success in the past are not sufficient for thriving in the future.

One day, while browsing the Internet, I came across an article in *Business Insider* with the headline "Blockbuster's CEO Once Passed Up a Chance to Buy Netflix For Only $50 million." I was surprised to learn that in 2000 the co-founder and CEO of Netflix, Reed Hastings, had approached the former Blockbuster CEO, John Antioco, and wanted to sell Netflix for $50 million. Obviously, it appeared that Antioco wasn't leading from the future. He failed to see the emerging trends of video on-demand and online streaming, which had begun to disrupt the way we consume videos. Antioco perceived Netflix to be a "very small niche business" and ended the negotiations. According to another online article, in *Variety*, "Epic Fail: How Blockbuster Could Have Owned Netflix," senior editor Marc Graser stated, "Blockbuster chiefs lacked the vision to see how the industry was shifting under the video rental chain's feet." The article quoted a former high-ranking Blockbuster executive who stated, "But management and vision are two separate things." The executive was cited as saying, "We had the option to buy Netflix for $50 million and we didn't do it. They were losing money. They came around a few times." Why was the Blockbuster leadership team blind to the emerging patterns of disruption in the video market?

Blockbuster's eventual demise came in 2010, when the organization filed for Chapter 11 bankruptcy protection. Ironically, this was not only due to challenging losses and millions in debt, but due to competition from Netflix and Redbox on-demand services. Blockbuster did not realize their business model was being threatened until Netflix tapped into streaming. It was too late; Blockbuster filed for bankruptcy and Netflix profits rose to the billions.

The demise of Blockbuster reinforces the notion that leaders must lead from the future. Leaders must embrace and deal with complexity, learn from diverse perspectives, and pursue potentials. Leaders must become strategic thinkers. The future is not a big event waiting to arrive; it is already here and it is constantly evolving. The visions and growth goals you created must constantly evolve to remain relevant. The current era calls for leaders to operate with a future-oriented mindset.

Digital Disruption: The New Way of Life

Leaders must not remain blind to the digital transformation. There is evidence of disruption everywhere and it's the theme that characterizes the digital age. Disruption is defining and redefining the standards and protocol by which individuals and businesses function. It is a core concern for executives; it's forcing them to re-think their business model and operate with an eye on the future. We enjoy many benefits of digital disruption, such as streaming music on our smartphones, conducting meetings in the cloud, the digital workplace, and wearable electronic devices. Disruption is here to stay and will continue to accelerate.

What does this mean to you, as a leader who has crafted a well-defined strategy and clear growth goals? As you execute your plan, the decision-making process must be agile as you sense and scan the future to detect emerging trends and patterns. Foresight must drive insight and the corresponding actions must be agile. Flexibility and agility are required in leading from the future.

Connectedness is driving social change and innovation in the mobile economy. This economy is a battlefield for the hearts, minds, and dollars of many people. In this mobile economy, we are organized as a global community, which influences events, drives business profitability, and defines the future. Global strategist Parag Khanna, in a talk presented at a TED conference, shared:

> "The global connectivity revolution, in all of its forms—transportation, energy and communications—has enabled such a quantum leap in the mobility of people, of goods, of resources, of knowledge, such that we can no longer even think of geography as distinct from it. In fact, I view the two forces as fusing together into what I call "connectography."

We are rising above geographical constraints, choosing where and when to shop and engage in conversations.

As technology, globalization, and socio-economic factors continue to change and "shrink" the world we live in, leaders must constantly evolve and adapt to these changes to remain relevant. Thriving in the digital age requires shifting from the traditional forms of leadership and embracing competencies that will enable us to be futuristic, operate with clarity,

respond quickly, and be able to see the big picture. To lead from the future, I recommend that leaders should intentionally focus on, and develop core leadership competencies. These competencies are the ability to be:
- Visionary
- Resilient
- Adaptive
- Creative

Visionary
Seeing Beyond the Ordinary

"All human situations have their inconveniences. We feel those of the present but neither see nor feel those of the future; and hence we often make troublesome changes without amendment, and frequently for the worse." —Benjamin Franklin

Visionary leaders will see beyond the ordinary and create a vision of where they want to be in the future, growing their business of life or organization. Leaders will master effective communication, to articulate the vision and inspire investors, suppliers, employees, and others to support the vision.

Seeing beyond the ordinary requires leaders to nurture a spirit of boldness and curiosity, with their eyes fixed on the destination. Visionary leaders will focus on, and consider the big picture, and look beyond the current scene. To lead from the future, visionaries anticipate impending changes, and operate in a proactive (rather than reactive) mode.

Visionaries will accept challenges; however, their focus will be on leveraging opportunities.

The investor and philanthropist Sir Richard Branson is an example of a visionary leader. He became an entrepreneur at a tender age, starting his first business venture (*Student* magazine), and later opened the chain of Virgin Megastores. He entered the airline industry by focusing his attention on an opportunity rather than a problem during a trip to Puerto Rico. The flight he was on was cancelled and Sir Richard seized the opportunity to charter his own plane, allowing the other stranded passengers to pay a small fee to cover the cost. This gave rise to the birth of the airlines known as Virgin Atlantic Airways and Virgin Australia. Sir Richard entered the airline business because of his ability to see a challenge and envision a solution in the midst of uncertainty.

Visionaries see from diverse perspectives and encourage others to embrace creativity and innovation. In September 2014, Sir Richard entered the unmanned aircraft systems industry, investing in 3D Robotics, a drone company. He believes in affordable technology, and envisions that this will enable more people to view the world from different perspectives. This kind of vision for the future defines visionaries, who are forward-thinking and aspirational. To lead from the future, you will need to see through likewise lenses, seize opportunities, create new visions, be comfortable with change, and evolve your personal growth as the world evolves.

Techniques to Foster Visionary Leadership

Developing your capabilities as a visionary leader is not a far-fetched idea. Here are some techniques I use to enhance my visionary competency.

- *Value diversity in culture and thoughts.* A crystal is a transparent prism that is impacted by externalities such as light. Exposure to natural, colored, or white light will cause the crystal to refract the light and emit brilliance. The angle and intensity of light (the externalities) can alter the brilliance of the crystal. Perspectives from externalities such as diverse cultures are crucial for enlightenment. Embracing diversity will open your eyes to re-examine the status quo, and to see new possibilities. Diversity in culture, thoughts, and processes will facilitate the emergence of multiple perspectives to the same problem. Begin to see the value in diversity and intentionally seek to learn about different cultures.

- *Leverage collective intelligence.* Your intellectual capital is limited to your base knowledge. Collective knowledge utilizes the sense-making capabilities of others to create new meaning and introduce new data patterns to help you anticipate change. Enhance your visionary competency by building strategic relationships to gain access to a broader collective intelligence.

- *Dial down your activities.* Your mind is a powerful resource, but innovation and creativity will remain in your subconscious if your mind is never given the opportunity to pause and listen. Invest in the time to dial down your activities and allow revolutionary ideas to emerge from your subconscious thoughts to the forefront of your mind. Quarterly, I dial down and disconnect from the ebb and flow of the business of life to listen to my thoughts. I assess all goals and actions, listen to the voice of change, then apply problem-solving to innovate new ways of doing and being. Make a promise to invest in the time to regularly dial down.

- *Enhance your communication skills.* There are many investors and supporters who are resourceful and accessible. To gain their buy-in, leaders must share their vision in simple language. Practice using simple language to share your vision and gain buy-in.

- *Refresh your vocabulary.* Visionaries generate the best ideas and implement innovative solutions because they engage in the art of questioning. They consistently seek to understand why and why not. Add "Why?" and "Why not?" to your vocabulary. These words serve the purpose of removing limitations and breaking down walls of impossibilities to develop solutions for complex challenges.

- *Acquire industry knowledge.* At the center of every vision (personal, leadership, or business) lies knowledge. Be curious about the latest industry news. Invest the time to read industry news through online or print publications, articles, and industry networks. The knowledge you acquire will trigger insight and foresight for predictive analysis, observation, and decision-making.

Resilient
Advancing Despite Adversity

"What lies behind you and what lies in front of you, pales in comparison to what lies inside of you." —Ralph Waldo Emerson

The road you travel on to execute your growth goals will be filled with setbacks and adversities. Will you bounce back from disappointments or crumble under the pressures in this business of life? The ability to bounce back is a test of your resiliency. The world is fast-paced and disruptive, and to lead from the future, leaders must be resilient. They must be able to quickly bounce back from setbacks and prevail over disruptions. Leaders who are resilient do not nurture failure; they accept and seek to understand it. They leverage the value and lessons learned from hindsight to envision the future. Resilient leaders will not be overwhelmed by setbacks or changes. They will draw on their visionary competencies and inner strength to bounce back and respond to changes.

Henry Ford, founder of Ford Motor Company, revolutionized the American transportation industry. Ford manufactured the Model T automobile, which was the first vehicle affordable enough to be accessible to middle-class American families. He was committed to systematically lowering cost, which led to a franchise of dealerships in North America and in other countries. However, before Ford's success with the Model T, he had unsuccessful vehicle manufacturing ventures.

Ford founded Detroit Automobile Company and later dissolved it because the automobiles produced were of lower quality and higher price than he desired. He later designed and built a 26-horsepower automobile and collaborated with stockholders from Detroit Automobile Company to form the Henry Ford Company. Concerned with staffing additions, he left the company bearing his name. Despite setbacks and failures, Ford was resilient and found a way to continue. He was committed to lifelong learning, releasing the past and seeing opportunities in challenges.

Ford explored new ventures and formed a partnership, Ford & Malcomson Ltd., to manufacture inexpensive automobiles. He never allowed his vision to die. He leased a factory and contracted a machine shop to supply parts but suffered a financial crisis due to slow sales. The resilient Ford and his partners bounced back by engaging new investors and convincing their supplier, the Dodge Brothers, to accept a portion of the new company, which we now know as Ford Motor Company.

Ford was a resilient leader and failure was not an option; neither was the status quo. He leveraged hindsight and insight from failed business ventures, drew on his visionary competency, and took risks to achieve his ultimate vision.

Leading from the future means you will take risks, try new things. Resilient leaders will not focus on failures; they will focus on their vision. Resiliency will enable you to draw from your strengths and move forward, with your purpose at the forefront of your mind. Resilient leaders will advance despite adversity because they have confidence in their intellectual and psychological assets. During encounters with adversity, strengths are leveraged. Adversity is viewed as an opportunity for personal growth and to close intellectual or psychological gaps. Without resiliency, you will not be able to survive and thrive in the digital age, where adversity and change is normal.

Techniques to Foster Resilient Leadership

Leading from the future includes fostering resiliency, so that you can advance despite adversity. Here are some techniques I use to develop my resilient competency.

- In the face of adversities, stay in tune with your sense of purpose. Understand your personal why and remain grounded by staying connected to your faith and spirituality.

- Self-awareness plays a significant role in developing your resilience competency. Remind yourself of your strengths, knowledge, values, and be confident in your abilities. You will draw from these assets when you encounter challenges.

- Practice optimism in every situation. Optimism is not the absence of adversity. Practicing optimism means engaging your thought patterns to focus on the opportunities and leveraging hindsight to understand what contributed to the adversity. It means being aware of the capabilities you use to navigate difficult periods. Optimism means having a mindset in adverse situations that believes what lays ahead is bigger and brighter than what lies behind.

- Don't wait for challenges to occur to develop problem-solving skills. My family and I frequently drive and explore North America. My husband, Rufus, enjoys ignoring the GPS and driving on unknown roads to reach our destinations. Rufus appointed himself as the "pilot" and referred to me as the "co-pilot." One day I inquired into the reasons for the detours; truth is, I was scared because it was late at night and only trees were visible. He responded, "There may be a day when the known route is no longer accessible and I must detour and find another route to get to our destination." I got it! In the event of a road detour, Rufus would be capable of detecting alternate solutions in a rational manner. Problem-solving skills are essential during crisis. Experimenting with different problem-solving techniques will build up your confidence and help you develop emotional self-management skills.

Adaptive
Staying in the Game

"The Internet is becoming the town square for the global village of tomorrow." —Bill Gates

The personal and business space you operate in is experiencing a constant flow of rapid, complex, and disruptive changes. Answers are unknown and resolving challenges requires the acquisition of new information and innovation. Adaptability is far-reaching and extends beyond digital disruptions to include cultural, emotional, procedural, and cognitive adaptations.

These changes require adaptive leadership approaches where leaders are capable of understanding the environment, foreseeing opportunities, innovating, and adapting to the changes. Leaders cannot afford the luxury of just coping with change. New dreams and fresh ideas demand change. To chart new courses, leaders will need to navigate a space that is changing. Rigid structures are of the past and flexibility is the present. Leaders must be willing to experiment, take risks, adapt during uncertainties, and develop solutions. Adaptive leaders must constantly look outward and question what they are seeing, then use their insights to re-align their vision with the changing environment.

When a vision is misaligned with the current reality,

creative tension will emerge. Creative tension, if not managed appropriately, may result in your vision being abandoned. Leaders will need to demonstrate emotional self-management and adapt cognitively to resolve the tension using diverse approaches. Do not use your creative energy to focus on negativity. To stay in the game, use your creative energy to anticipate trends and envision novel ideas.

The great leader known as Moses was responsible for leading the former Egyptian slaves through the wilderness into a new land based upon a covenant made with God. For Moses, this was both a vision and a command that presented a powerful illustration of adaptive leadership. As Moses embarked on the long journey through the hot wilderness, he encountered many challenges for which he was unprepared. Moses embraced change and accepted the risks. Undaunted by the uncertainties ahead, Moses led the Israelites on the journey towards their destination—the Promised Land.

Moses wandered in the desert for forty years. He did not know this part of the plan. He did not know the people would demand bread to eat, and he had no ready-made solution. When Moses took a long time to return from the top of Mount Sinai, he did not know the people would become impatient and rebellious. When Moses finally reached the Red Sea, he did not know ahead of time, that he would look behind and see the Egyptian army pursuing them. In a complex and uncertain situation, Moses was faced with an army behind him and a sea before him. There was no apparent way of escape or obvious solution.

In each uncertain situation, Moses remained adaptive.

Reaching the Promised Land seemed impossible but he demonstrated emotional self-management. Moses was optimistic in every uncertain situation and tapped into his dependable support system. He trusted God to collaborate, co-create, and innovate with him. Manna was provided when the Israelites needed bread. The waters of the Red Sea were parted to the sides, and the Israelites escaped the perils of the Egyptian army. Moses demonstrated adaptive leadership by guiding the Israelites through several experiences of learning, changing, re-envisioning, and adapting during periods of uncertainty.

Techniques to Foster Adaptive Leadership

Leading from the future requires you to be adaptable, flexible, and capable of managing uncertain and unpredictable environments. Below are techniques that I have used and continue to leverage.

- *Think outside the box.* This is more than a business cliché. There is always a better way of thinking, conceptualizing, and doing. The contents of the box typically include: traditions, standard operating procedures, routines, status quo, and best practices. Eventually these contents become outdated, unproductive, and ineffective. To think outside the box, there has to be a shifting and a moving away from the normal way of doing things. Train yourself to think beyond traditional ways of analyzing problems. Shift your focus from the challenge, change the rules, re-arrange the norms, plan backwards, and play the game in a different way. Changing the rules will interrupt the thinking pattern of your brain. Your brain will sense the shift, observe the change, re-train, and produce new patterns of thoughts. Thinking outside the box is an intentional attitude. If you chose to remain in the box, your ideas and solutions will remain the same and set you on a path of becoming irrelevant.

- *In the VUCA world, become comfortable with uncertainty.* Instead of fearing uncertainties, embrace them and begin to explore the why to gain understanding. In the uncertainties are breakthroughs for your business of life. Complex challenges require new learning. Nurture an experimental mindset to discover new ideas and test potential solutions. Eventually, uncertainties will yield to understanding, and understanding will reveal opportunities for change and growth.
- *Be authentic.* In *Hamlet*, William Shakespeare penned the now famous line spoken by Polonius as he bid his son Laertes farewell: "This above all: to thine own self be true. And it must follow, as night follows day, thou canst not be false to any man." Polonius gave his son one of the best pieces of fatherly advice: practice self-awareness and be true to who you were created to be. Authentic leaders are in tune with their emotions, and appropriately engage strategies for emotional self-management during times of change. Authentic leaders are bold and stand strong in confidence and power: power to choose; power to listen; power to influence;

power to own their voice and express their thoughts; power to create and power to adapt. Conduct personal SWOTs repeatedly to enhance your self-awareness and build your confidence.
- *Develop a support system.* Adaptive leadership includes being able to mobilize a team to problem-solve. Establish a support structure consisting of mentors, coaches, strategic advisors, and professional colleagues. During times of uncertainty and complexity, they will become the voices of wisdom, insight, foresight, and innovation.

Creative
Fueling Innovation

> "Capital isn't so important in business. Experience isn't so important. You can get both these things. What is important is ideas. If you have ideas, you have the main asset you need, and there isn't any limit to what you can do with your business and your life." —Harvey Firestone

In today's digitally driven economy, innovation is critical for organizations and leaders. Organizations are leveraging idea-generation consulting agencies to help create innovative cultures. Leading from the future and fostering innovation requires creativity, the fuel of innovation. In this digital age, organizations view a creative leader not as one who has all the ideas but as one who possesses the ability to foster creative cultures where ideas can flow, and where novel innovative solutions will emerge. Gay Mitchell, in the role of Executive VP, HR, Royal Bank, stated, "Companies have to nurture [creativity and motivation]—and have to do it by building a compassionate yet performance-driven corporate culture. In the knowledge economy, the traditional *soft* people side of our business has become the new *hard* side." Creativity should not only be viewed as a soft skill but as a hard (intellectual or cognitive) skill, relevant and important in the digital age. This is an unusual way of thinking. This is creativity.

In the context of this business of life, creativity means being a leader who possesses the analytical ability to sort through the chaos and complexity of the VUCA world. You possess the capabilities to move beyond traditional ideas and concepts, sort volumes of data to find the patterns and themes to generate ideas, and create meaningful unique solutions. Creativity not only ignites innovation but gives rise to an entrepreneurial spirit. As you lead from the future, creativity will allow you to refresh your vision and keep your growth goals relevant. Your creative mindset should always question if there is a different and more current approach to achieving the desired outcomes. As creative leaders listen to the future, they will focus on the insights that will disrupt any status quo in their growth goals.

In your business of life, leading from the future calls for co-dependency across core leadership competencies. A critical aspect of creativity is power in diversity. Innovation is not possible without creativity, and creativity requires collaboration. You may have heard the phrase "the whole is greater than the sum of its parts." The creative process requires you to embrace collaboration and diverse perspectives, and to share and exchange information. This is the reason your vision must be compelling, and you must operate with a growth mindset to attract the right diverse creative team to help with the attainment of your vision.

Techniques to Foster Creative Leadership

Leading from the future requires a creative mind. Here are techniques I consistently use to develop my creative leadership.

- *Unplug from the VUCA world and plug in to the master Creator.* Creativity will flow when you take time to silence the noise from the VUCA world and create the space for the inward creative gift to flow outward. You were gifted with creativity at birth and wired with ideas. The ideas that lie dormant inside you will awaken when you pause to listen to the instructions of your heart and the voice of Wisdom.

- *Similar to unplugging from the VUCA world, allow your brain to rest.* The information being transmitted from the VUCA world comes quickly and fights to gain your attention. Information overload may cause distractions and a shift in focus. Best-selling author and pharmaceutical business tycoon Alan Cohen wrote, "There is virtue in work and there is virtue in rest. Use both and overlook neither." Minimize the information overload from the VUCA world, and rest your brain to enhance creativity and increase your productivity.

- *Walk to boost your thoughts.* Ever since I discovered the power of walking I have integrated at least ten to fifteen minutes of power-walking daily. There are many who believe creativity is at its highest peak during walks because walking boosts inspiration and creative thinking. Steve Jobs, the late co-founder of Apple, was known for conducting walking meetings. Daniel L. Schwartz and Marily Oppezzo of Stanford University conducted a research to determine the effect of walking on creativity. The researchers placed participants in different environments (such as walking, and sitting indoors and outdoors); based on the findings they concluded that walking had a positive impact on creativity. Get up and get walking!

- *Be committed to taking action.* Many great leaders, such as Sir Richard Branson, Dr. Pat Francis, Steve Jobs, Dr. Martin Luther King, and Henry Ford, have a common leadership quality: a commitment to taking action. They have instigated personal actions and inspired others to become involved in their vision. They challenged the status quo, re-envisioned the future, and believed in shaping, influencing, and impacting the world they live in. They did not sit on the sidelines waiting for change to happen; they became and continue to be stories of change. They are status quo disrupters. Maintaining the status quo is a killer of creativity, while being action-oriented helps foster creativity. In graduate school, one of my professors would encourage us: "Start anywhere. Go anywhere." I encourage you to develop your creative competency by starting anywhere today: take action and become a story of change.

The world is changing and your business of life must become a continuous cycle of releasing the past, managing the present, listening, sensing, and leading from the future. The decision to remain relevant is within your power. Will you make the decision and invest in yourself today, to pursue personal mastery and growth? Big dreams don't just happen; every leader must intentionally design their business of life.

NOTES

Chapter 1: Pursuit of Personal Mastery
1. Short, R. R. (1998). *Learning in relationship: Foundation for personal and professional success.* Seattle, WA: Learning in Action Technologies.
2. Jessica Cox. (2017, June 18). In Wikipedia, The Free Encyclopedia. Retrieved 19:26, July 4, 2017, from https://en.wikipedia.org/w/index.php?title=Jessica_Cox&oldid=786260928
3. Senge, P. M. (2006). The Fifth Discipline: The Art and Practice of the Learning Organization. New York, NY: Currency Doubleday.
4. Carl Jung Quotes. (n.d.). BrainyQuote.com. Retrieved January 29, 2018, from BrainyQuote.com Web site: https://www.brainyquote.com/quotes/carl_jung_146686
5. George Washington Carver Quotes. (n.d.). BrainyQuote.com. Retrieved January 29, 2018, from BrainyQuote.com Web site: https://www.brainyquote.com/quotes/george_washington_carver_386067

Chapter 2: Re-Think the Status Quo

1. Unknown Quotes. (n.d.). BrainyQuote.com. Retrieved January 29, 2018, from BrainyQuote.com Web site: https://www.brainyquote.com/quotes/unknown_133991`
2. Martin Luther King, Jr.. (n.d.). AZQuotes.com. Retrieved August 31, 2017, from AZQuotes.com Web site: http://www.azquotes.com/quote/614712
3. Hiner, J. (2011, October 6). Here's to the Crazy Ones. Retrieved from http://www.techrepublic.com/blog/tech-sanity-check/video-steve-jobs-narrating-heres-to-the-crazy-ones-tribute/
4. Dugan, A., Nelson, B. (2017). 3 Trends That Will Disrupt Your Workplace Forever. Gallup Business Journal. Retrieved from http://www.gallup.com/businessjournal/211799/trends-disrupt-workplace-forever.aspx
5. Travis Bradberry Quotes. (n.d.). BrainyQuote.com. Retrieved January 29, 2018, from BrainyQuote.com Web site: https://www.brainyquote.com/quotes/travis_bradberry_734922
6. Robert Kiyosaki Quotes. (n.d.). BrainyQuote.com. Retrieved August 30, 2017, from BrainyQuote.com Web site: https://www.brainyquote.com/quotes/quotes/r/robertkiyo626875.html
7. Simon Sinek Quotes. (n.d.). BrainyQuote.com. Retrieved January 28, 2018, from BrainyQuote.com Web site: https://www.brainyquote.com/quotes/simon_sinek_568117

8. Jochen Zeitz Quotes. (n.d.). BrainyQuote.com. Retrieved January 28, 2018, from BrainyQuote.com Web site: https://www.brainyquote.com/quotes/jochen_zeitz_720903
9. Retrieved from http://www.coca-colacompany.com/stories/coke-lore-new-coke
10. Reprinted with permission of the publisher. Theory U, copyright© 2009 by C. Otto Scharmer, Berrett-Koehler Publishers, Inc., San Francisco, CA. All rights reserved. www.bkconnection.com
11. Martin Luther King, Jr.. (n.d.). BrainyQuote.com. Retrieved January 28, 2018, from BrainyQuote.com Web site: https://www.brainyquote.com/quotes/martin_luther_king_jr_105087
12. Sturgeon, J. (2012, January 14). Where Nortel went wrong. *Financial Post* Retrieved from http://business.financialpost.com/technology/where-nortel-went-wrong/
13. Eleanor Roosevelt. (n.d.). AZQuotes.com. Retrieved August 31, 2017, from AZQuotes.com Web site: http://www.azquotes.com/author/12603-Eleanor_Roosevelt

Chapter 3: Re-New Your Mind

1. Marilyn Ferguson Quotes. (n.d.). BrainyQuote.com. Retrieved January 29, 2018, from BrainyQuote.com Web site: https://www.brainyquote.com/quotes/marilyn_ferguson_151854
2. Retrieved from http://www.thequotablecoach.com/tag/john-mcdonnell/

3. Washington Irving Quotes. (n.d.). BrainyQuote.com. Retrieved January 29, 2018, from BrainyQuote.com Web site: https://www.brainyquote.com/quotes/washington_irving_122774
4. Senge, P. M. (2006). *The Fifth Discipline: The Art and Practice of the Learning Organization*. New York, NY: Currency Doubleday.
5. Napoleon Hill Quotes. (n.d.). BrainyQuote.com. Retrieved January 29, 2018, from BrainyQuote.com Web site: https://www.brainyquote.com/quotes/napoleon_hill_101794
6. Harvey S. Firestone Quotes. (n.d.). BrainyQuote.com. Retrieved January 29, 2018, from BrainyQuote.com Web site: https://www.brainyquote.com/quotes/harvey_s_firestone_158289
7. Madonna Buder. (2017, May 5). In *Wikipedia, The Free Encyclopedia*. Retrieved 19:30, July 4, 2017, from https://en.wikipedia.org/w/index.php?title=Madonna_Buder&oldid=778844482
8. Lao Tzu Quotes. (n.d.). BrainyQuote.com. Retrieved January 29, 2018, from BrainyQuote.com Web site: https://www.brainyquote.com/quotes/lao_tzu_130742
9. Alexander Graham Bell Quotes. (n.d.). BrainyQuote.com. Retrieved January 29, 2018, from BrainyQuote.com Web site: https://www.brainyquote.com/quotes/alexander_graham_bell_408695

10. Nik Wallenda. (2017, August 12). In Wikipedia, The Free Encyclopedia. Retrieved 04:28, August 29, 2017, from https://en.wikipedia.org/w/index.php?title=Nik_Wallenda&oldid=795204227
11. ABC NEWS (Producer). (2012). Nik Wallenda's Niagara Falls Megastunt [DVD]. Available from http://abcnews.go.com/Nightline/video/nik-wallendas-niagara-falls-megastunt-16583602
12. Goleman, Daniel, Richard Boyatzis, and Annie McKee. (2002). *Primal Leadership: Unleashing the Power of Emotional Intelligence.* Boston, MA: Harvard Business Press Books.
13. Alexander Graham Bell Quotes. (n.d.). BrainyQuote.com. Retrieved January 29, 2018, from BrainyQuote.com Web site: https://www.brainyquote.com/quotes/alexander_graham_bell_409116
14. Eckhart Tolle Quotes. (n.d.). BrainyQuote.com. Retrieved January 29, 2018, from BrainyQuote.com Web site: https://www.brainyquote.com/quotes/eckhart_tolle_571602
15. Retrieved from http://emilysquotes.com/if-you-truly-want-to-change-your-life-you-must-first-be-willing-to-change-your-mind/
16. George Bernard Shaw Quotes. (n.d.). BrainyQuote.com. Retrieved January 29, 2018, from BrainyQuote.com Web site: https://www.brainyquote.com/quotes/george_bernard_shaw_386923

Chapter 4: Re-Envision Your Future

1. Jim Rohn Quotes. (n.d.). BrainyQuote.com. Retrieved January 29, 2018, from BrainyQuote.com Web site: https://www.brainyquote.com/quotes/jim_rohn_165075
2. Goleman, Daniel, Richard Boyatzis, and Annie McKee. (2002). Primal Leadership: Unleashing the Power of Emotional Intelligence. Boston, MA: Harvard Business Press Books.
3. Albert Einstein Quotes. (n.d.). BrainyQuote.com. Retrieved January 29, 2018, from BrainyQuote.com Web site: https://www.brainyquote.com/quotes/albert_einstein_130625
4. Retrieved from http://www.thequotablecoach.com/at-the-end-of-each-day-you-should-play-back-the-tapes-of-your-performance-the-results-should-either-applaud-you-or-prod-you/
5. Denis Waitley Quotes. (n.d.). BrainyQuote.com. Retrieved January 29, 2018, from BrainyQuote.com Web site: https://www.brainyquote.com/quotes/denis_waitley_146914
6. Confucius Quotes. (n.d.). BrainyQuote.com. Retrieved January 29, 2018, from BrainyQuote.com Web site: https://www.brainyquote.com/quotes/confucius_136804
7. Brian Tracy Quotes. (n.d.). BrainyQuote.com. Retrieved January 29, 2018, from BrainyQuote.com Web site: https://www.brainyquote.com/quotes/brian_tracy_125752

8. Ralph Waldo Emerson. (n.d.). AZQuotes.com. Retrieved January 29, 2018, from AZQuotes.com Web site: http://www.azquotes.com/quote/876955
9. Reprinted with permission of the publisher. From *Leaders Make the Future*, copyright© 2012 by Bob Johansen, Berrett-Koehler Publishers, Inc., San Francisco, CA. All rights reserved. www.bkconnection.com
10. John F. Kennedy Quotes. (n.d.). BrainyQuote.com. Retrieved January 29, 2018, from BrainyQuote.com Web site: https://www.brainyquote.com/quotes/john_f_kennedy_121068
11. Alan Cohen. (n.d.). AZQuotes.com. Retrieved August 31, 2017, from AZQuotes.com Web site: http://www.azquotes.com/quote/591617
12. Brian Tracy Quotes. (n.d.). BrainyQuote.com. Retrieved January 29, 2018, from BrainyQuote.com Web site: https://www.brainyquote.com/quotes/brian_tracy_163247
13. Senge, P. M. (2006). *The Fifth Discipline: The Art and Practice of the Learning Organization*. New York, NY: Currency Doubleday.

Chapter 5: Re-Define Your Goals

1. Mark Caine Quotes. (n.d.). BrainyQuote.com. Retrieved January 29, 2018, from BrainyQuote.com Web site: https://www.brainyquote.com/quotes/mark_caine_122102

2. Doran, G. T. (1981). "There's a S.M.A.R.T. way to write management's goals and objectives." *Management Review*. AMA FORUM. 70 (11): 35–36.
3. Zig Ziglar Quotes. (n.d.). BrainyQuote.com. Retrieved January 29, 2018, from BrainyQuote.com Web site: https://www.brainyquote.com/quotes/zig_ziglar_120890
4. Pareto principle. (2017, October 1). In *Wikipedia, The Free Encyclopedia*. Retrieved 00:16, November 15, 2017, from https://en.wikipedia.org/w/index.php?title=Pareto_principle&oldid=803225225

Chapter 6: Leading from the Future

1. Fujitsu. (n.d). Fit for Digital. Co-creation in the Age of Disruption Findings: Retrieved from http://www.fujitsu.com/global/Images/Fit-for-Digital_Report.pdf
2. Chong, C. (2015). Blockbuter's CEO once passed upon a chance to buy Netflix for only $50 million. *Business Insider*. Retrieved from http://www.businessinsider.com/blockbuster-ceo-passed-up-chance-to-buy-netflix-for-50-million-2015-7
3. Graser, M. (2013). Epic Fail: How Blockbuster Could Have Owned Netflix. *Variety*. Retrieved from http://variety.com/2013/biz/news/epic-fail-how-blockbuster-could-have-owned-netflix-1200823443/
4. Blockbuster LLC. (2017, July 26). In *Wikipedia, The Free Encyclopedia*. Retrieved 20:15, July 26, 2017, from https://en.wikipedia.org/w/index.php?title=Blockbuster_LLC&oldid=792361433

5. Khanna, P. (2016). How megacities are changing the map of the world [DVD]. In TED Ideas worth spreading. Available from https://www.ted.com/talks/parag_khanna_how_megacities_are_changing_the_map_of_the_world
6. Benjamin Franklin. (n.d.). AZQuotes.com. Retrieved January 30, 2018, from AZQuotes.com Web site: http://www.azquotes.com/quote/536522
7. Richard Branson. (2017, July 27). In *Wikipedia, The Free Encyclopedia*. Retrieved 21:39, July 28, 2017, from https://en.wikipedia.org/w/index.php?title=Richard_Branson&oldid=792591682
8. Center for Creative Leadership. (n.d). Adaptability: 1 Idea, 2 Facts, 5 Tips. Retrieved from https://www.ccl.org/articles/leading-effectively-articles/adaptability-1-idea-3-facts-5-tips/
9. Ralph Waldo Emerson Quotes. (n.d.). BrainyQuote.com. Retrieved January 29, 2018, from BrainyQuote.com Web site: https://www.brainyquote.com/quotes/ralph_waldo_emerson_386697
10. Henry Ford. (2017, November 17). In Wikipedia, The Free Encyclopedia. Retrieved 23:17, November 17, 2017, from https://en.wikipedia.org/w/index.php?title=Henry_Ford&oldid=810720022
11. Bill Gates Quotes. (n.d.). BrainyQuote.com. Retrieved January 29, 2018, from BrainyQuote.com Web site: https://www.brainyquote.com/quotes/bill_gates_384628

12. Scripture taken from the New King James Version®. Copyright © 1982 by Thomas Nelson. Used by permission. All rights reserved
13. Retrieved from https://www.leadershipnow.com/creativityquotes.html
14. Alan Cohen. (n.d.). AZQuotes.com. Retrieved November 20, 2017, from AZQuotes.com Web site: http://www.azquotes.com/quote/743955
15. Oppezzo, M., & Schwartz, D. L. (2014). Give your ideas some legs: The positive effect of walking on creative thinking. *Journal of Experimental Psychology: Learning, Memory, and Cognition, 40*(4), 1142–1152. https://doi.org/10.1037/a0036577

GLOSSARY

Creative Tension: The gap that occurs when current reality is different from a vision.

Dimension: An area of your life that you focus on when you are creating a personal vision statement. These areas include faith, health, family, wealth, personal growth, education/career, relationships, business, community, and leadership growth.

Emotional Tension: Negative emotions that arise because of creative tension.

Growth Goals: A synergy that exists between goals and your personal growth that ensures the achievement of short-term, long-term, and life goals, with the ultimate culmination in clear visions and purposeful living.

Intellectual Assets: Cognitive elements that relate to your ability to think and understand. Examples include knowledge and skills.

Leader: An individual who is responsible for creating, shaping, and designing their future, regardless of their positional authority within an organization.

Methodology: A set of practices, processes, methods and procedures used to accomplish a set of objectives.

Open Heart: The capacity for empathic listening, for appreciative inquiry, and for exchanging places with another person or system.

Open Mind: The capacity to suspend judgment, see something with fresh eyes, inquire, and reflect.

Personal Mastery: A lifelong discipline of personal growth and learning.

Psychological Assets: Positive emotions and competencies that impact the mind and create a mental state conducive to success. Examples include optimism, confidence, hope, and a growth mindset.

Social Technology: A communications platform or capability that is used to foster and facilitate social interactions, such as peer coaching and networks.

Voice of Judgement: Old and limiting patterns of judgement and thought.

VUCA: A world characterized by Volatility, Uncertainty, Complexity, and Ambiguity.

WHAT IS YOUR STRATEGY FOR
PERSONAL, LEADERSHIP AND BUSINESS GROWTH?
DO YOU HAVE AN EFFECTIVE PLAN?

Avril Riley Enterprise has developed an individual and group coaching for sustainability program inspired by her many years of experience and latest book, Big Dreams Don't Just Happen.

In the digital age investing in yourself is not an option, it is a necessity of life.

REMAIN RELEVANT! DAILY INVEST THE TIME TO GROW AND DEVELOP.

ELEMENTS OF THE PROGRAM INCLUDES:

- Digital Vision Board
- Personal SWOT Analysis
- Map of Peaks and Valley
- Idea Generation Sessions
- Digital Assessment Coaching
- Personal Change Management
- Setting and Managing Priorities
- Personal Development Planning
- Leadership Development Planning
- Business Development Planning
- Perspective Power Cluster™ Mentoring

What do you get? Growth Journal with an executive goal growth plan.

Bonus: 120 minutes coaching during execution of your goal growth plan.

LIFE YOUR VISION. LIVE YOUR PURPOSE.

Contact Avril Riley to get started now!
Email: avril@avrilriley.com
Call: 905.840.4591
www.avrilriley.com
©2017 Avril Riley Enterprise